BASICS

ANIMATION

04

Barry Purves

stop-motion

Ethical: aware-
ness/
reflect-
ion/
debate

:a

An AVA Book
Published by AVA Publishing SA
Rue des Fontenailles 16
Case Postale
1000 Lausanne 6
Switzerland
Tel: +41 786 005 109
Email: enquiries@avabooks.ch

Distributed by Thames & Hudson (ex-North America)
181a High Holborn
London WC1V 7QX
United Kingdom
Tel: +44 20 7845 5000
Fax: +44 20 7845 5055
Email: sales@thameshudson.co.uk
www.thamesandhudson.com

Distributed in the USA & Canada by:
Ingram Publisher Services Inc.
1 Ingram Blvd.
La Vergne TN 37086
USA
Tel: +1 866 400 5351
Fax: +1 800 838 1149
Email: customer.service@ingrampublisherservices.com

English Language Support Office
AVA Publishing (UK) Ltd.
Tel: +44 1903 204 455
Email: enquiries@avabooks.ch

ISBN 978-2-940373-73-4

10 9 8 7 6 5 4 3 2 1

Design by Tamasin Cole
www.tamasincole.co.uk

Production by AVA Book Production Pte. Ltd., Singapore
Tel: +65 6334 8173
Fax: +65 6259 9830
Email: production@avabooks.com.sg

Cover image: Madame Tutli-Putli (2007). Photo used with
permission of the National Film Board of Canada.

Max & Co 2007

directors
Frédéric Guillaume and
Samuel Guillaume

Two beautifully stylised puppets
with their characters easily
discernible through costume
and posture.

Contents

So what exactly is stop-motion? These days an exact answer is bound to be a little imprecise as most animation techniques contain some elements and principles that overlap others, but stop-motion could be generally defined as creating the illusion of movement or performance recorded over successive exposed frames of film by manipulating, usually by hand, some solid object or puppet or cut-out image in a spatial physical setting.

If any of that excites you, we're on our way.

▶

She-Bop 1988

animator
Joanna Priestley

Joanna Priestley uses her animation to take the viewer through bold, almost shamanistic transformations.

Other techniques follow the same process but with a succession of drawings or with computer-generated (CG) images. Motion is created when the camera is stopped – that's a very satisfying contradiction, especially when considering that this movement is purely an illusion. There is no literal movement. Technically, that definition could apply to all film, as what we are watching is, in effect, just a series of still images. The film has paused in front of the projection beam for a fraction of a second, before being replaced by a subsequent image, with a black frame in between. If the images are close enough in appearance the brain links the two images, giving the impression of a continuous movement. Even the crystal clarity of digital projection relies on this combination of still images and black frames.

Stop-motion animation is slow and laborious and to make even a very short film demands a huge amount of resources, patience and unflagging energy. Yet students still jump at the chance to work in this oldest of mediums and at any animation exhibition it will always be the physical puppets that draw the crowds, with the public instinctively reaching out to touch them. The fact that the characters actually exist is one of the main satisfactions and the intrigue of an inanimate object 'magically' moving is never likely to lose its appeal.

Most audiences are aware enough to tell whether what they are watching started life in a computer or as a solid object. This is not just due to tell-tale marks in the sculpting such as fingerprints, nor the texture of the fabrics, but more due to the very distinct way the characters move.

Stop-motion is not the slickest or the smoothest of animation. CG claims that credit, but this is part of the appeal of stop-motion. What some people see as failings, others get passionate about. I love the quirkiness of stop-motion, the certain roughness suggesting a human hand has been intimately and directly involved, with the emotional resonances that that brings. I love the trick of seeing a solid object move in real space, watching the unexpected ways the light interacts over the materials. I love an object being given an apparent life. I love the trick. There is something shamanistic about it, as well as something that connects immediately to childhood games and, perhaps, to darker fantasies. The very physicality of stop-motion makes all these accessible.

Throughout this book we'll explore these particular qualities of stop-motion so that your first film really does exploit all that is good and glorious about this very special film-making technique, particularly with reference to the more narrative and figurative or puppet-led films. We'll also explore other disciplines, other forms of puppetry and other mediums that share a joyous celebration of artifice with stop-motion to see how they tell their stories and what we can learn from them.

Hopefully by the time we finish you'll be eager and equipped to get started, and will enjoy stop-motion as much as I and so many others have.

▼

The Pigeon 2009

animator
Hywel Prytherch Roberts

The manipulators, the animators, of this stop-motion character are totally invisible to the audience, their work done between frames.

What is stop-motion?

In Chapter 1 we'll explore how stop-motion is different from other techniques, how it evolved and how it has been used.

Focusing the idea

In Chapter 2 we'll consider the various narrative strengths of stop-motion and how these can be applied to your ideas.

The puppets

In Chapter 3 we'll look at the wide range of puppets available to stop-motion animators and consider how they might help you to tell your story.

Preparations

In Chapter 4 we'll examine how all the other elements of film-making, such as set designs, costumes and colour schemes, can best be used with stop-motion.

Tools and techniques

In Chapter 5 we'll look at how all of the elements of stop-motion affect the storytelling and the film itself and how they are just as important as the animation.

Movement and performance

Finally, in Chapter 6 we'll consider how to make the most of the very distinctive movement of stop-motion.

How to get the most out of this book

This book introduces the different elements of the art of stop-motion, from developing the initial concept and selecting a suitable puppet right down to creating a mood and lighting your set. Each chapter provides numerous examples of work by leading animators, with quotes to give an insight into their rationales, methodologies and working processes. Key animation principles are isolated to help show how they are applied in practice.

Section headings
provide a clear strapline to allow you to quickly locate areas of interest.

Page numbers
are located on the top right corner of each spread.

Vocal performances

However you use dialogue, it is essential that it is recorded and broken down into frames on the **bar sheets** long before filming. An animator can fit loose mouth shapes to the dialogue much more easily than an actor can fit his or her voice to already filmed animation.

When recording the voices for stop-motion, the trick is to get as much physicality and spontaneity into the voices as possible, as well as an absolute awareness of the geography of the scene. Most animators will enjoy picking up on all the little breaths and pauses; seeing a puppet apparently stuttering over a word brings it to life. Anticipating a piece of dialogue by animating an intake of breath adds a surprising amount of life. Once again, it is the little unplanned imperfections that work so well.

A cold mechanical voice, treated almost as a voice-over, will not sit comfortably with the puppet. It is therefore vital to describe as best you can to the actor what the puppet will be doing; for example, are they running along a beach or whispering in a cupboard?

Any physical dynamics will only help the animation. It is important to encourage the actors to breathe life into the words with what they feel works, and where at all possible, it helps to have the cast for that scene in the same space looking at each other, so that the rhythm flows naturally. If this is not possible, have someone reading the lines off microphone so that you never have an actor performing their lines in isolation. Technically it's wise to leave a gap between each line of dialogue, but sometimes you can hear the actor anticipating that break so this should be treated on a case by case basis.

Of course, all this can mean that the animation performance has to, out of necessity, fit round the vocal performance. This can be inhibiting to the animation, therefore in an ideal world the animator will have some input with the voice work (such as suggesting certain bits of character business or physical actions that will affect the vocal performance). Try to make sure the dialogue and music is available on your work station as you shoot, so you can hear every accent and pause each frame. Refer to it as much as possible.

△ ▷
**Gilbert & Sullivan –
The Very Models** 1998
animator
Barry Purves
Mr Sullivan in full song. Though he had no tongue and no teeth, following the strong rhythm of the music and versatile mouth shapes made for convincing lip-synch.

Bar sheets, or x sheets/dope sheets. These sheets contain the dialogue or music broken down into accurately timed sounds spanning numerous frames, helping the animator choreograph the action or mouth shapes. This is an essential visualisation of sound, showing the rhythms and silences. It is our equivalent of a musical score.

Tools and techniques

Sound > **Dialogue** > Special effects

Glossary
provides the definitions of key terms highlighted in the main text.

Captions
provide additional information and directives about how to read the illustration, or historical context.

Chapter navigation
highlights the current unit and lists the previous and following sections.

Stop-motion

Illustrations

appear throughout to provide insight and information to support the main text.

Sets

Credibility

If a set is too clean and flat then it can easily disrupt the illusion of scale. Texture, stop-motion's great friend, can help mitigate this effect. Introducing some essential weathering to the sets can also help. Sets need to look lived in and you'll be surprised what a difference a bit of shading in corners or the odd scratch can make. The same applies to costumes. As always, it's the little unexpected touches and imperfections that make a set and a character credible to the viewer.

For this reason, animators usually prefer working on real sets, where we can respond to the environment and introduce tiny but telling details. Working in a green screen vacuum is exactly that – a vacuum. It's harder to feel part of the scene, and to some extent the animation becomes like a layer of a cel animation or an element in a CG film. Time and time again we come back to enjoying stop-motion because it is all there right in front of us and we can touch it. Being part of this small world it is not hard to imagine how the characters respond and behave.

A whole new world

As every single item has to be created from scratch, why not enjoy giving the sets character and style? Sets, like all the other elements of your film, should contribute to and reflect the overarching story, characters and themes. When you are designing, try to create a whole new credible world for the story, where everything works seamlessly together. For example, remember that stop-motion sets often don't need to match the proportions of real human architecture. This is simply because the characters are often animals or other fantasy creations with a wide range of anatomical proportions. If a door is designed for human proportions, the chances are it won't fit all the characters in your film.

Much of the success of the Wallace and Gromit films depends on the details in the sets, which are often only apparent in repeated viewings. Consider how much the dog bones on Gromit's wallpaper say about him. Just as there is often a visual shorthand for puppets (such as haughty characters being portrayed by tall, spiky puppets) so the colour and shapes used in sets can be reflective of the stories they tell. Of course, however fanciful you get with the sets, it's essential that the characters stand out in front. The sets support the characters, not the other way round.

▲
Electreecity 2008

animators
Sarah Davison and
Sarah Duffield-Harding

A beautifully stylised, simple and imaginative set. This scene makes creative use of texture, and gives a familiar image of a tree a fresh perspective.

Tip: Doors

Remember that there will be elements on the set that will need to be animated at specific times, such as doors, but for the rest of the scene they need to be rock solid. Magnets can help with this or small hinges that can be tensioned. Nothing ruins a shot more than a character walking towards a door, and the door twitching before it is opened. This is usually caused by the animator's clumsiness. Everything has to be fixed solidly to the set, and yet still be free to move as necessary. Solving this requires ingenuity and to enjoy stop-motion it certainly helps to enjoy this kind of problem solving.

> I always laugh when I hear that a form of animation is dying. They've been saying for years that stop-motion is dead. But a few of us are still around.
>
> Mike Johnson

Preparations

Working with others > **Sets** > Costume

Quotes

from featured animators throughout history are included.

Thinking points

summarise, direct and inform particular approaches to practice and analysis.

Introduction > **How to get the most out of this book**

In this opening chapter we will look at how stop-motion evolved almost by accident in the early days of cinema. We will also look at what exactly stop-motion is as well as how it works and its pros and cons. We'll explore the uniquely tactile process of stop-motion, how this differs from other animation techniques and why the process is such an important part of the end result. We will consider the many different ways in which the technique has been used over the years and how it may develop in the future.

Finally, we'll consider how to best use this particular technique for your own films.

◀

Clash of the Titans 1981

animator
Ray Harryhausen

Here we see one of the greats of stop-motion animation, Ray Harryhausen, animating the fearsome Kraken. In some scenes this model is intercut with an underwater live-action model.

The beginnings

In late nineteenth-century Paris Georges Méliès was using invisible wires, trap doors, sheets of glass, smoke, and complex automata to become a master of spectacular theatrical illusion and magic. Part of his act involved playing a film on stage, and he made these movies himself. As he was filming some material in the street his camera jammed for a few seconds. This simple accident changed everything, for him and for us, as on the developed film the jump cut had seemingly transformed an omnibus into a hearse – a delicious conceit for Méliès. The camera glitch had recreated a version of one of Méliès' substitution tricks, where on stage he might replace a woman with a skeleton through the use of a trap door and a swirl of a cloak. This simple trick had been recreated by accident through the camera stopping; by stopping motion.

Visual tricks

This basic technique, of course, still forms the basis of all stop-motion today. We are constantly substituting one move for another move, or a smaller object by a bigger object to look as though things are growing, or swapping different mouth shapes. However, Méliès did not leave the innovation there. Instead he began to experiment with all manner of cinematic ideas and built a huge production studio to produce effects such as seemingly disembodied heads floating against black velvet backgrounds (using the same idea as blue/green screen), moving backgrounds, **pixilation** and so on. He used these new developments in cinematic technology to create extraordinary fantasy worlds.

▶

Cinderella 1899

animator
Georges Méliès

A still from the Georges Méliès film *Cinderella* shows his love of the fantastic. His films are full of such extraordinary figures and living skeletons. Skeletons in particular are a recurring theme in animation – it is after all, about giving life to that which does not have life.

Pixilation is a technique used in film where real people are manipulated a frame at a time, often alongside animated objects, giving a movement close in feel to stop-motion.

While his contemporaries, such as the Lumière Brothers, were recording everyday events, Méliès was thrusting film into absolute fantasy. He used themes of devils, history, fairy tales and space travel, and also sometimes recreated scenes the documentary cameras missed – such as a scene of the actual Coronation of Edward VII. Interestingly, he also used his tricks to sell commercial products, something most animators fall into at some point. His inventiveness and problem solving were astonishing, and he embodied the inquisitive quality that every animator needs.

As animators we are confronted every day with different challenges to achieve certain illusions. It's therefore apt that Méliès was a magician and showman, as to be a stop-motion animator you'll certainly need to be a bit of both. Stop-motion isn't really about mathematics and facts and figures, but is much more about performance, tricks, illusions and instincts. Méliès only seldom used pure stop-motion as such, as in *Cinderella* (1899), but he used it as a means of achieving his fantastical visions. He may not have invented stop-motion as we know it today, but he certainly kick-started it into life.

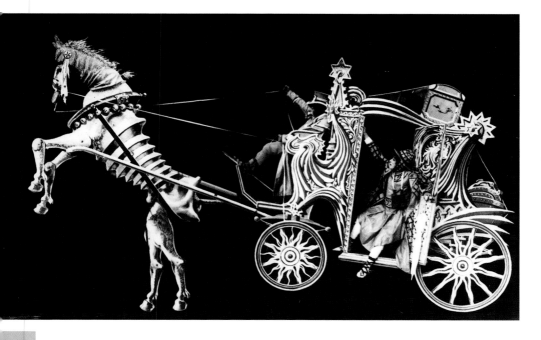

Other early stars

Méliès didn't appear, like one of his tricks, out of nowhere. His work was the result of decades, maybe centuries, of worldwide experiments with optical toys, the new film cameras and general advances in technology; but to many animators, he is very much the spirit of stop-motion. Significant contemporaries of his included Edwin Porter in America who used stop-motion to bring beds to life in *Dream of a Rarebit Fiend* (1906). A year later, J. Stuart Blackton manipulated objects in stop-motion to suggest haunted house activity in *The Haunted Hotel* (1907) while Émile Cohl had fun with dancing matches in *Bewitched Matches* (1913).

These films all used stop-motion as a special effect but the pure manipulation of puppets started to appear in such films as Ladislaw Starewicz's amazing animal and insect led films from Russia: *The Tale of the Fox* (1930), for example, and *The Mascot* (1934). These films contain extraordinarily sophisticated and complex animation, with very detailed puppets. The sheer number of them would defeat many an animator today. Above all the puppets were acting and, in many cases, thanks to some sophisticated mechanics, seemingly breathing.

Whereas such films as these feature completely fabricated miniature worlds, in 1933 Willis O'Brien gave the impression that his masterful creation, King Kong, was rampaging through a very real live-action world. Even today, *King Kong's* mix of techniques and special effects remains hugely impressive, but it is the little details of psychological performance and character that still touch us. For example, Kong's moment of doubt as he flicks the dead T-Rex's jaw still raises a smile. This small gesture showed a puppet was capable of acting.

**The Tale of the Fox
(Le Roman de Renard)** 1930

director
Ladislaw Starewicz

This early film, with exquisite and surprisingly expressive puppets, was one of the very first times that stop-motion was used to create a performance rather than a special effect.

What is stop-motion?

The illusion of movement

Stop-motion animators create a moving performance between frames without ever being seen themselves, creating the illusion of independent continuous movement. In the past this illusion has been attributed to a theory called 'persistence of vision'.

Many film-makers and animators refer to persistence of vision as a phenomenon whereby the human eye (and/or brain) always retains images for a fraction of a second. The theory is that everything we perceive is a combination of what is happening right now and what happened an instant before. Film-makers often credit this process for allowing viewers to perceive a sequence of individual frames as a continuous moving picture.

However, there is currently no medical evidence to support this theory and psychologists contend that persistence of vision is not necessary for the success of film motion. This is, of course, different from the familiar experience of seeing an 'after-image' after looking at a relatively bright light. The persistence of vision theory asserts that this process happens constantly for everything we see, and it is this which is now widely questioned.

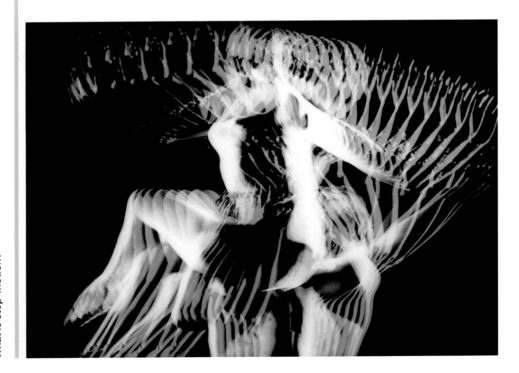

Edgar Allan Poe

In this inventive live puppetry performance by the Center for Puppetry Arts, Atlanta the manipulator and the process of manipulation are part of the piece. The action takes place in real time in front of an audience.

Pas de deux 1968

animator
Norman McLaren

A still from Norman McLaren's groundbreaking film *Pas de deux*, using many consecutive images of a dancer in motion condensed into a single frame. The validity of the persistence of vision theory is something of a minefield and is these days usually dismissed. It has been suggested that if the theory was correct then we would see the world as it appears in this innovative film.

Exercise: Puppetry

Stop-motion combines the relatively modern world of animation with the ancient tradition of puppetry. What makes stop-motion different from most other forms of puppetry is that it is not performed or filmed in real time, nor is it played in front of an audience and, unusually for puppets, the operators are not seen.

Try to find as many different examples of puppetry as possible and see how the various techniques help or hinder the character's movement. See how the technique is used in the storytelling.

The beginnings > The illusion of movement > Physicality

Continuous movement

In stop-motion, as with all animation, the successful creation of continuous movement depends on how one frame, or one position, relates to the previous and subsequent frames. The more a frame connects to the previous one, in terms of composition, movement, colour and so on, the better and more credible the flow of the animation.

If two sequential frames have no relation to each other, the viewer's brain will struggle to make sense of the information being presented. They will certainly not perceive any illusion of smooth movement. For example, if in one frame an object is positioned left of frame and in the next frame the object has moved slightly to the right – the viewer's brain can easily make the assumption that the object moved that bit to the right. There is a subconscious assumption that the object has taken the most direct path between the two positions. However, if the second frame showed the object to the extreme right of the shot the viewer will not have enough information to assume a smooth movement; there is no link between the object's positions.

To let the viewer perceive fluid movement we need to help as much as possible to create this illusion. Let's continue to use our object moving from left to right across the screen as an example. If we want to create the illusion that the object has curved from the left of frame to the top of frame and then down to the right, then we must give the movement as much detail as possible. This needs more information and more frames – typically showing the interim movements at a rate of around 24 or 25 frames per second (fps). An identical movement in live action would also have a trailing blur to suggest the direction of movement. In stop-motion animation, depending on budget and technology, we don't usually have that blur and so need to really spell out every bit of movement. We can do this by over-emphasising elements in the animation and how the environment reacts to the character's movement.

Cityco Christmas Campaign
2009

director
Barry Purves

This sequence of stills from a recent lively commercial shows the increments between successive frames. Working with large numbers of objects and puppets, all moving at different speeds, certainly requires concentration and an awareness of spatial choreography.

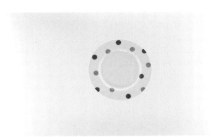

1

2

3

4

5

6

7

8

Helping the eye read animation

In a nutshell, the smoothness or otherwise of your animation depends on how much connected detail and information you can put into it.

In everyday life there can be excessive information that cannot be processed. For example, too much unconnected detail caused by a rapid head movement, too much bobbing up and down or a lack of focus can all lead to disorientation and dizziness, sometimes alleviated by the eye blinking or just closing the eyes. The eye will usually blink, at the start of a quick head turn, to avoid having to deal with too much information on a move that looks like a **whip pan**. People on a roller coaster will be travelling too fast to make sense of what is rushing by, and will therefore feel totally disorientated (or worse). The eye cannot make sense of everything quickly enough. Focusing on the static handrail in front makes things easier.

Similarly, in animation we find that if there is a wild and frantic piece of animation to be choreographed it helps to counterbalance this with a gentle, more controlled piece of animation elsewhere in the frame. This is no different to playing the piano. The right hand usually does all the more animated parts, while the left hand plods along lending a solid grounding to the piece. Take away the beat, or through line, of the left hand and the right hand seems less focused.

A static counterpoint

Often, to make a movement work, the viewer needs to see something not move – a lovely contradiction. If an animated character were moving against a blank background in flat lighting, the effect of its actual movement would not read as well as if there were dappled lighting and a background with detail. The movement registers by contrasting against something that is not moving. This particularly applies to stop-motion where characters are moving in a real space.

It is important to make the absolute most of the movement to make it easy for the viewer's eyes and brain to perceive what we want them to perceive. If the animation includes too many quick cuts or overly large or small movements, it just won't '**read**' properly to the viewer. We have to be over-emphatic with the storytelling moments that communicate what that movement is about.

Achilles 1996

animator
Barry Purves

Here a strong pose emphasising the storytelling moments of a movement is helped by a trailing tail that gives the illusion of momentum and inertia. Our animation is all about illusion not accurate reproduction.

The beginnings > The illusion of movement > Physicality

Whip pan is when a camera moves from one position to another at such a speed that the viewer does not register what is between the two positions.

Read, in this context, means to understand or register the meaning or significance of what is seen.

Transcending realism

Animation techniques such as 2D drawn, working with clay and computer-generated (CG) animation are all able to suggest the weight and inertia of movement through stretching and squashing the characters. However, working with solid puppets can mean we have to find various little tricks to make the movement come across clearly to the viewer. We'll look at these later, but it's worth noting here that over-emphasising movement starts to take animation, certainly stop-motion animation, away from merely copying live action. Instead it becomes a whole new way of communicating and this is to be encouraged and relished. What works for a live-action actor does not necessarily work for a stop-motion puppet and this requires a different approach, which is actually a real joy and liberation. If you have the sensibilities of a dancer, a mime or an actor, all of whom thrive on movement that's more about storytelling than reality, then you are likely to find stop-motion a real pleasure.

His Dark Materials 2009

author/puppets
**Philip Pullman/
Blind Summit Theatre**

A scene from a Blind Summit Theatre production where rather than copying real life through invisible technique, the joy of the illusion and the artifice is magnificently on display.

▲

Next 1989

animator
Barry Purves

The dangling, trailing arms and
hanging head of the dummy give
a decent suggestion of weight in
a puppet that weighed very little.
It can be beneficial to clearly
show the laws of physics at
work even in a fantastical scene.

One of the main attractions of stop-motion is that the animator is handling something very physical that's moving in a concrete space, reacting with spontaneity to light and focus and depth. In other forms of animation shadows have to be added, but in well-lit stop-motion shadows happen naturally and give an absolutely credible existence to the characters. The viewer can see the character responding to its environment, and existing in it. The puppet is directly connected to its world, which can only help the believability of its narrative.

Texture and lighting

With physical characters comes texture, another great asset of stop-motion, and we can make the most of it with effective lighting. There's little point in sculpting a gloriously detailed puppet, or sets and backgrounds, then flattening out all the textures with very dull uniform front lighting. The character would then start to look like a cartoon. You may have seen low-budget or lazy cartoons where characters are not affected by the lighting designs on the background art. As a consequence the characters pass through their environment without causing shadows or any other physical effects and do not really connect with the world around them.

That said, however, CG animation is now capable of producing extraordinarily photo-realistic textures on its characters. CG can give its animal characters beautiful fur with even a suggestion of muscles underneath that stop-motion can't even contemplate. This is made possible as a result of many decisions, vast effort and much coordinating between the riggers and the texture and lighting artists. With stop-motion, once you have the puppets and the space, you're halfway there. As stop-motion animators we can enjoy the fact that once the puppets have been sculpted, all the effort of making them look connected to their world happens for free. As we'll see throughout the rest of the book, there are also a variety of little tricks to further secure a character in their world.

Rigoletto 1995

animator
Barry Purves

A character from *Rigoletto* who looks very much a part of his environment – as he is. This is due to the careful lighting and the fact that he is physically present in the set and not composited or added in at a later stage. He is a real object in a real space and the viewer absorbs that information, taking clues from how the shadows fall, which helps anchor the puppet in space.

Detail

The detail possible on puppets often takes an audience by surprise, and again this is a quality we should relish. Deciding on the little details of puppets and their environments can be one of the most enjoyable elements of our craft. Including a wealth of small details also helps provide the viewer with additional information about the scale of the figures and sets, giving the characters a history and personality, locating them in their world. Small, well-thought-out details can also make repeated viewings enjoyable.

Including a similar level of detail in drawn animation could be frustrating and extremely labour intensive – although not impossible. Imagine having to reproduce the bristling fur of an animal or a patchwork of a costume every frame.

To some extent, drawn animation works by capturing as much of a character with as little detail as possible, making every drawn line reveal something. Every line is there for a reason.

However, some drawn animation contains an inordinate amount of detail, but the sheer effort and control of reproducing complex faces, for example, can lead to inaccuracy in the lines. This inaccuracy gives the lines a 'life of their own', making them waver and fidget. This produces a very lively effect, as in many of Joanna Quinn's vibrant and fleshly films; very different from the precise outlines of most drawn animation. The nearest we can get to this joyous energy in stop-motion is with clay animation when the animator is quite loose with the sculpting.

▶

Puffer Girl 2009

animator
Joan Gratz

Joan Gratz pioneered the animation technique known as claypainting. This involves working with bits of clay to blend colours and then etching fine lines to create a seamless flow of images. In this short film, *Puffer Girl*, the technique moves into the digital realm by incorporating photography, Photoshop and AfterEffects.

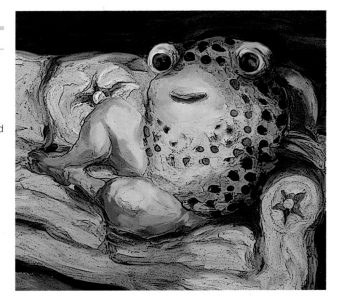

What is stop-motion?

▲ ▶

Wife of Bath 1998

animator
Joanna Quinn

Joanna Quinn's gloriously fleshly *Wife of Bath* film uses a lively and spontaneous line – the human hand is very evident in the technique. The movement in the line gives the characters so much energy; in effect giving them life. The detail in the characters also separates them easily from the looser, less important backgrounds.

Faces

Animators working with puppets are lucky that once a face has been sculpted, that detail is there for good. However, if you are working with Plasticine or clay a complicated face does still require a lot of work to maintain. Should you sculpt a character whose face is full of interesting wrinkles it will be extremely difficult to maintain these through the physical process of handling and resculpting the character. Claymation is different to other forms of stop-motion as it requires resculpting between frames rather than just repositioning. The soft, malleable material is easily marked with fingerprints and dirt and the smoothing and cleaning needed for each frame can slow the animation process. As a clay animator, it is essential that you are a competent sculptor and enjoy the qualities of clay.

Watch one of Aardman's Wallace and Gromit films, focusing particularly on Gromit's face. It is deceptively simple, with a strong, clean and very distinct shape that the animator can reproduce and maintain easily from frame to frame. Expression comes mainly from his eyes and eyebrows, as well as some well-timed blinks and a sensational use of body language and rhythm. The secret of Gromit is that he is very controlled, so that every little movement says something.

Harvie Krumpet 2003

animator
Adam Elliot

A still from Adam Elliot's heartbreaking film *Harvie Krumpet*, dealing with huge and sensitive issues, all conveyed through a deliberately simple character design, in which the material and the sculpting is a conscious part of the storytelling.

The Wrong Trousers 1993

animator
Nick Park

Wallace and Gromit, enjoying the exaggerated features, textures and material that define their characters. Strong, clean shapes in clay and Plasticine are easier to maintain during the constant resculpting than more detailed characters.

Recommended viewing

It is well worth watching Garri Bardin's *Grey Wolf and Little Red Riding Hood* (1990). Here the sculpting does not have the finesse of Gromit, but it does have a mad energy that suits its kinetic form of storytelling. The resculpting is a conscious feature in its own right. Similarly, in Adam Elliot's sensitive films, some of the joy is in seeing the manipulation of the Plasticine itself. Adam's animation works, ironically, by how little it moves – take a look at his remarkable film *Harvie Krumpet* (2003) to see just how effective this can be.

The illusion of movement > Physicality > A continuous performance

Most animation goes through several processes, with different elements being animated at different times, or by setting the key positions first, and then filling in with in-betweens. Stop-motion has none of that, and works with a direct, intimate through line. You literally start at frame one of a shot, and finish with the last frame, organically shaping the shot as you go. This linear method of shooting (sometimes known as straight-ahead animation) helps the action flow. It is also a very satisfying and logical way to film. It is a continuous performance in small chunks and, assuming you are the only animator touching the puppet, this leads to strong continuity in the performance.

Personality transfer

With this intimacy between puppet and animator certain characteristics of either can be transferred. With a puppet in his hand, the animator is likely to get the most direct and honest response in the animation. There's no technology, no one else to get in the way. This can occasionally be a drawback, with the animator's personality colouring the animation too much, especially on a major project where a role will be shared by several animators. Mostly, however, it is a benefit and animators are often cast for certain types of scenes. For example, some find slapstick scenes easier, while others cope better with more emotional scenes. It would be a shame not to let the personality of the animator emerge through the puppet. As with other forms of puppetry, it is important to revel in the direct contact between puppet and puppeteer. The contact between a human hand and the puppet gives the animation so much soul, for lack of a better word.

Puppet and puppeteer

The very direct relationship between puppet and puppeteer is shown here by animator Michael Cusack (left) and his star, the Gargoyle; and puppeteer Ronnie Burkett with his character Billy Twinkle (facing page). With stop-motion, as with traditional puppetry, it is often the unpredictability of the human interaction with a physical object that gives the characters so much spirit.

Animating 'live'

Most stop-motion audiences enjoy its quirkiness, its little imperfections. Similarly, most animators enjoy the fact that when animating you don't get the chance to refine. Once you have repositioned a character, you have immediately lost the previous frame. This is both a huge pressure and also part of the excitement. This is as near to acting and to animating live, with all the adrenalin and thrill that that implies, as it is possible to get. It can make you feel very naked and exposed. How you react to that pressure must colour how you feel about stop-motion.

Although your first short film might be achieved largely single-handedly, on larger projects you are likely to be part of a team. In stop-motion most of the crew tends to be in the same studio space; this is unlike CG animation where, sometimes, much of the work is farmed out overseas or to other studios, and the internet used to view the progress. Stop-motion cannot practically be farmed out as there's much sharing of puppets and sets, and it is created by a group working together on the same project, with communication very much part of the process. There is a lot of sharing and encouraging and critiquing involved – there's a supportive team spirit and camaraderie that is rarely found in other animation techniques.

Tomorrow 2009

animator
Bob Lee

Animator Bob Lee filming *Tomorrow* in very cramped conditions. Of all the animation techniques, only stop-motion is quite so physically demanding and uncomfortable.

Stop-motion is now most often used as a medium in its own right, and that's what we will focus on for most of this book. However, many of the techniques we now use in purely animated films, were developed over the years in which the technique was used as a special effect within live-action films. Let's take a look at how stop-motion allowed film-makers to introduce fantasy or action elements into their work when it simply couldn't be achieved any other way.

A practical solution

In the 1933 film of *King Kong*, Willis O'Brien's most famous creation was a mere 45cm (18 inches) tall but was pretending to be the size of a house. Stop-motion was used to create the illusion of this enormous beast as, of course, primates simply don't exist at that scale; nor could gorillas have been trained to act (as was initially suggested!). A man in a fur suit was even mentioned, but thankfully that idea was rejected too. Stop-motion allowed Kong to be performed with great nuances, and with a compelling physicality. In 1933, stop-motion was the best possible solution to the problem of bringing a fantasy creature to life on the big screen. However, in Peter Jackson's 2005 re-imagining of the story a motion capture performance was entirely appropriate. Modern audiences would not accept the distinct movement of stop-motion in such a visceral live-action film.

King Kong 1933

animator
Willis O'Brien

This much-loved and inspirational publicity poster is somewhat generous about Kong's size. In 1933 stop-motion was the most practical way to bring this fantasy creature to life. It allowed Kong to perform and thereby allowed the audience to truly engage with him as a character alongside the human actors in the film.

King Kong 2005

animator
Weta Digital

By 2005 technology and audience expectations had both moved on. This meant that Andy Serkis' motion capture performance and Weta Digital 3D animation were a far more suitable choice to make the modern day Kong believable.

Recommended viewing

Have a look at a moment immediately after King Kong has killed the T-Rex in the 1933 version of the film. As the dinosaur lies still after the visceral fight, Kong gently plays with its limp jaw, as if making sure he has killed it. Suddenly among all the violence is a tender piece of character performance. There is a thought process and a special effect becomes a performance. It is such an iconic moment that it was referenced in the 2005 version.

A continuous performance > Special effects > Wholly animated films

Stop-motion stunt work

Stop-motion has also pretended to be live action in stunts that were too dangerous for the actors to perform themselves – or when the logistics were just too complicated and expensive to do it for real. For example a short, almost invisible shot in *The Adventures of Baron Munchausen* (1989) has a puppet of John Neville as the Baron sat astride a huge cannonball flying through the air, much as there had been puppets of Fay Wray in the 1933 *King Kong*. Similarly, the animated runaway mine cart sequences in *Indiana Jones and the Temple of Doom* (1984) obviously saved on the building of a huge set. In the same film, the lowering of an animated Kate Capshaw into a fiery pit saved the actress certain discomfort. However, because of stop-motion's quirkiness and the sophistication of CG, such sequences now look slightly awkward within the rest of the film.

Many early films used stop-motion for characters, such as a stop-motion Buster Keaton on a dinosaur in *Three Ages* (1923), but it was also used in combination with model sets of fantasy landscapes, or sets that could not be built full scale in a studio. Across these sets, often further enhanced by beautifully painted matte paintings of castles or dramatic scenery, stuttered live-action model trains or stop-motion vehicles crashing, usually with a very static human character inside.

In old horror films you'll find stop-motion killer tree vines or skeletons. It does pop up in surprising places. Much of Hitchcock's early films are full of miniature work. Whenever an effect couldn't be done any other way due to scale or budget, stop-motion was often spliced into live-action films. To a modern audience these scenes simply look awkward, with the scale betrayed all too easily through a different feel to the focus, or the lighting or the movement. Elements such as fire, water and smoke notoriously look unconvincing when used with miniature models. The water droplets are simply too big and do not behave the same way as large expanses of water. This is where CG imagery has superseded stop-motion. It can make these effects utterly convincing.

The Dam Busters 1955

A still from *The Dam Busters* showing miniature model work combined with live action. In many early films stop-motion elements, such as crashing vehicles and planes or collapsing buildings, were the only way to suggest these special effects.

Futuristic machinery

The AT-AT walkers in *The Empire Strikes Back* (1980) were small stop-motion models filmed to look like huge machines. Today they would almost certainly be created as CG models, with much more control and finesse (although an army of fans would miss their very distinctive walk and the fact they did actually exist as detailed models). These AT-AT machines, like the two-legged ED-209 machines in *RoboCop* (1987) and some of the underwater vehicles in *The Abyss* (1989), were trying to be realistic in a live-action film because it would have been very difficult to integrate them into the action in any other way. Real full-scale models could have been built and controlled with miles of cables, but the cost would have been prohibitive. Stop-motion models were a practical answer – the human hand doing away with the need for complex machinery.

In films such as *batteries not included* (1987) the main characters of small flying saucers are performed through a combination of stop-motion models against blue screen and live-action models on wires or rods. In this kind of film, if a miniature model needs a smoother movement than is usually possible with stop-motion, the model can sometimes be moved by external rods attached to motors during the actual exposure of the frame. This technique, known as 'go-motion', leads to a blurring of the action to create a more fluid move than traditional stop-motion.

The Empire Strikes Back
1980

animator
Phil Tippett

The AT-AT walkers from
The Empire Strikes Back were
beautifully animated by Phil
Tippett. Slow pacing and a
heavy rhythm gave the stop-
motion the illusion of immense
scale and heaviness, while also
giving a very distinct feel to
the movement.

Bringing fantasy to life

The beautifully performed dinosaurs and creatures of Jim Danforth, David Allen, Ray Harryhausen and Randall William Cook do now look solid next to the CG imagery of films such as *Jurassic Park* (1993). Digital technology allows every scale or ripple of muscles under the skin to be animated, even over-animated, and every hair can glisten with sweat. Computer graphics make it possible to achieve incredibly detailed characters and realistic movement, and issues such as suggesting the scale of these creatures is scarcely a problem.

In contrast, even the most sophisticated stop-motion is noticeable when placed alongside live action. There is something about the focus, the lighting, and especially the movement that betray their small scale. However, on many occasions we are very grateful for that. As a stop-motion Raquel Welch clings gamely from the claws of a pterodactyl in *One Million Years BC* (1966) most audiences do not for one moment forget the impressive technique needed for the illusion, but that does not hamper their enjoyment of the film. It even increases it.

Similarly Talos and the skeletons, from the sublime *Jason and the Argonauts* (1963), still stand up magnificently, as the stop-motion movement is highly appropriate for the fantastical figures of an awkward heavy statue and skeletons. However, creatures such as Pegasus and Calibos from *Clash of the Titans* (1981) have fared less well. This is largely because the switch between live action and stop-motion equivalents in consecutive shots stretches the illusion almost to breaking point. The stop-motion and sculpting are still hugely impressive but are simply comparably less credible when seen alongside live action and it is therefore understandable that the 2010 remake uses CG to create the fantasy creatures. However, if you took the 1981 creatures and put them into a wholly model world they would still be brilliant. Regardless of how advances in animation technology might colour the modern audience's perception of these films, the astonishing creations of Ray Harryhausen and co. remain stunning achievements and some of the most influential and most loved animation ever.

Medusa was fascinating to work with because I gave her a snake's body so that she could pull herself with her hands, which gave her a very creepy aura. I didn't want to animate cosmic gowns. Most Medusas you see in the classics have flowing robes which would be mad to even try to animate.

Ray Harryhausen

Jason and the Argonauts
1963

Clash of the Titans 1981 (right)

animator
Ray Harryhausen

The characteristic movement of stop-motion is so perfectly appropriate to imply the weight and size of a large, awkward metal statue like Talos (above). Similarly, Medusa's snake-like movement (right) creates a very sinister effect.

Wholly animated films

The most visible and celebratory use of stop-motion is in wholly animated films, when every prop, every costume, every character, every piece of set, have all been created in miniature scale. Every element of these films has the same design integrity. In wholly animated films such as *$9.99* (2008) the animation can really shine without the competition of live-action movement.

The unique movement and often heavily stylised and lit sets all complement each other, and all work together. Suddenly, in an appropriate context, the animation does not look awkward or second rate or inferior to live action, but is seen as something fitting and wonderfully quirky. It seems likely that films like this will continue to be made for a long time, whatever the advances in computer technology.

What people like about stop-motion animation is that it's real. It's like a magic trick, taking real things, real sets, and making them come to life with movement.

Joe Clokey

Stop-motion is now appreciated for its own, unique merits, as Wes Anderson's *Fantastic Mr Fox* (2009) demonstrated. It enjoyed and exploited all the idiosyncrasies and on-set effects associated with the technique.

Stop-motion no longer needs to compete with the sophistication of computers and so can now enjoy being low-tech. Certainly, there have been some excellent but deliberately low-tech commercials and short films with little more than roughly animated cereals or small toys or even chalk drawings on real walls. Audiences enjoy seeing and understanding the trick.

$9.99 2008

director
Tatia Rosenthal

Every element of this detailed film was created from scratch, allowing for a wonderful cohesion between the characters, props and sets.

Real-world settings

Another technique is to place an entirely animated cast of characters into a real-world setting. A recent, joyously inventive and provocative short film, *I Live in the Woods* (2008), by Max Winston, had the central character, a 30cm (12-inch) puppet, running along real country roads, climbing trees, and interacting with the environment; no mattes were necessary as the character was there in the same space. The moving shadows and flickering light add to the already enormous energy of the film. The scale of the puppet, in the context of the film, is never an issue. This film echoes the inventive cult BBC series from the mid-1960s called *The Pogles*, that saw small puppets animating running round real woods. The makers of this series, Peter Firman and Oliver Postgate, were also responsible for some wonderfully bizarre and much-loved stop-motion series, including *The Clangers* (1969–1974) and *Bagpuss* (1974).

The Pogles 1965–1968

animator
Oliver Postgate

Mr Pogle from the much-loved and groundbreaking BBC series with stop-motion puppets, initially, in real locations.

I Live in the Woods 2008

animator
Max Winston

Here Max Winston animates his character in a real setting in a raw, provocative film bursting with energy.

In Chapter 2 we will look at how the particular and quite extraordinary qualities of stop-motion lend themselves perfectly to certain stories and characters but may look inappropriate when used in other contexts.

We'll also consider how to make the most of these qualities and start to enjoy what stop-motion can bring to a film, as opposed to disguising it as an invisible effect. Finally we'll look at how the very physical and labour-intensive nature of stop-motion, and its budgets, can affect the storytelling.

A Christmas Dream 1946

director
Karel Zeman

In this classic film a young girl receives new, exciting presents for Christmas and so throws away her old rag doll. Santa then appears while the girl sleeps and makes her dream about the old doll coming to life and the two of them have an adventure together. Imaginative stories about dreams coming true and dolls springing to life are perfect for animation.

What is stop-motion? > **Focusing the idea** > The puppets

At the start of any project there must be a desire to tell a story, to suggest an idea or theme or to show something from a fresh perspective. How the story is told is as important as the story itself. However, although the technique of animation is certainly interesting in itself, that alone does not necessarily guarantee sufficiently captivating the audience – you must have something to say.

Adding to the technique

There have been great films whose *raison d'être* was to demonstrate the potential of a particular technique, but they are usually great because the narrative uses the technique rather than the technique using the narrative. You really do need a strong idea before approaching stop-motion, if only to justify the sheer effort involved.

You can't have animation without making a decision about the technique, which of course will affect every frame of the story. The technique of stop-motion is unavoidably part of the film, but it shouldn't be what the film is about. It has to be the tool that is the most appropriate way to tell a particular story, and that story must contain elements that could not be realised any other way.

Damaged Goods 2008

animator
Barnaby Barford

Damaged Goods tells a story
of love among the secret world
of discarded porcelain objects.
Their limited movement is part
of the appeal and part of the
characters' frustrations.

Exercise: Shop window stories

Have a look at three seemingly unlinked
objects in a shop window and try to make
a story or connection between them.
Find a character the audience will love
and establish relationships between the
three objects, and then find the drama
within the setting. Imagine what happens
in their secret world when the public aren't
looking. Or take two unrelated articles in a
newspaper and put the characters from
one in the context of the other and see
what happens. Can stop-motion make
these stories more interesting?

Stories and themes > Approaching the story

Rules of story-telling?

Although there are tricks, tips, formulas and devices for making stories work, there are no hard and fast rules to writing a story for animation, or for any other medium these days – but this was not always the case. The plays of the ancient Greeks were structured to follow the three unities laid down by Aristotle (384 BC–322 BC). These rules demanded that there be one main plot, one location and that all the action should take place within 24 hours. It was also suggested that the plays should include no more than two characters, and sometimes the chorus, on stage at any one moment. Following these rules gives the plays an enviable focus, and the economy certainly worked for the dazzling plays of the ancient Greeks, but those rules were eventually broken. Shakespeare, for example, very consciously acknowledged the rules and then ignored them. This is most obvious in the opening speeches of *Henry V*, which directly ask the audience to imagine many shifts of location and time and spectacle that couldn't be presented literally. This wasn't just a creative solution to budget constraints and limited resources. It was enjoying the artifice of the medium rather than being literal and functional.

Tip: Aristotle's three unities

These theatrical rules may be nearly 2500 years old but they can still be a useful focusing technique.

1   The unity of action dictates that a play should follow one main action and that subplots should be avoided.

2   The unity of place says that the action should be set in a single physical space and should not attempt to compress geography. The stage should not represent more than one place.

3   The unity of time says the action in a play should take place over no more than 24 hours.

Harvie Krumpet 2003

director
Adam Elliot

The Krumpets, from Adam Elliot's moving film, *Harvie Krumpet*, where a complex and tragic story is beautifully contrasted with the deliberately simplistic animation.

Focusing the idea

First, have a definite, clear practical ideal;
a goal, an objective. Second, have the
necessary means to achieve your ends;
wisdom, money, materials, and methods.
Third, adjust all your means to that end.

Aristotle

Harnessing imagination

Shakespeare's theatres were constructed to involve the audience; letting them use their imaginations by sharing the 'trick'. There was no **proscenium**, which can generate a 'them and us' feeling, as sometimes a cinema screen can. This can be a cold illusion, which becomes a barrier to the audience connecting with the piece.

Similarly, animation often works best when the action and characters are not presented as literal representations of reality. When we make the audience work to interpret what they see and hear, we help them to become involved with the process and thereby connect with and enjoy the storytelling. When an audience can share and contribute to this storytelling process then they become part of it.

Animation works most triumphantly when it acknowledges its artificiality and plays with its own tricks and limitations. This can be seen when little more than a metal box on caterpillar tracks, in *Wall-E* (2008), is able to suggest strong emotions, or when simple line drawings evoke recognisable situations or lumps of Plasticine create whole complex characters. A good way to test if your idea might revel in the artificiality of animation is to ask the question 'could this story be told better in live action?' If the answer is 'yes' then it may be time to think again. If the answer is 'no!' then the process of animation may truly add a new, engaging perspective to your story.

Next 1989

animator
Barry Purves

Audiences were encouraged to use their imaginations in Shakespeare's productions; they were aware of the artifice of theatre but still became involved in the action.

Focusing the idea

The **proscenium** is the part of a theatre stage in front of the curtain, which frames the action and hides the mechanics of how the production works.

▲

**The Nightmare
Before Christmas** 1993

director
Henry Selick

Tim Burton's *The Nightmare
Before Christmas* answers a
resounding 'no!' when asked if it
could have been done better in
live action. Every design choice,
every proportion and odd
movement is so appropriate
to animation, and especially
stop-motion.

The most important 'rule' in any form of storytelling is that you must keep your audience interested in your characters and situations. This requires the exploitation and thorough understanding of the medium in which the tale is told. It is possible to achieve prolonged audience interest through a whole range of techniques, including:

▶ Fast pacing

▶ Contrasting rhythms and increasing tension

▶ Exciting plots full of moments of **peripeteia** and suspense

▶ An unfolding mystery or constant revelations about the characters

▶ An escalating series of spectacle and effects.

However you choose to achieve it, it is vital that you keep the audience wanting to look at the screen, wanting to know what happens next. Stop-motion can be included as one of the elements that intrigue an audience but it is not a narrative element in itself.

Embracing artificiality

Whether it be animation or live-action film, most cinema, and the experience of watching it, is very artificial. The process of editing is a very unnatural process; our real lives do not jump from scene to scene and our eyes do not have a zoom function. Anything that is put on stage or film, by its definition, cannot be realistic, and certainly the notion of characters talking plot and dishing out back-story while playing to an invisible fourth wall or camera is very fake. Basically, any story that is told has some construction; it's theatrical, it's cinematic, it's mimed, it's fake and uses a barrage of tricks to keep the audience interested and in suspense. All the while it maintains some sort of credibility. Stories are not realistic. They are heightened versions of reality, using selective elements rearranged for maximum impact, and cutting out the bits that have no relevance.

Animation excels in this, being a medium where everything is fake and has to be created from scratch. It would be a waste not to exploit this artificiality.

Peripeteia is a sudden reversal of fortune or change in circumstances, especially in reference to fictional narrative.

▲

Life's a Zoo 2008

animator
Cuppa Coffee Studios

Here we see some animals
behaving badly. Using puppets,
especially as non-human
characters, allows storytellers
to say and do things that
people couldn't get away with.
It is one of the oldest tools of
storytelling – and it is still
enormously effective.

Animated stories

The best animated films are often those that enjoy their artifice. As animators we have the liberty to exploit all the elements of storytelling and design and movement and character to keep the viewer interested. Such liberty might be wasted on faithful representations of reality, but stories of secret worlds, fantastic creatures, skewed perspectives and stylistic innovation all thrive in animation.

Animation is a form of art and as such many films prefer to concentrate on a visual idea or technique, and not a narrative. Indeed many lauded films are little more than a succession of colours or shapes, some scratched directly onto the film – such as Richard Reeves' brilliant *Linear Dreams* (1997). Others focus on the texture of paint as it is applied, and who's to say this cannot be made interesting?

But if you are trying to develop a narrative in your film, it would be a shame not to enjoy the tricks of this medium. That does not necessarily mean filling your story with zombies, robots, dinosaurs or talking animals. But it does mean finding a fluid reality or a twisted perspective to your story. It's certainly helpful to have a central active character with whom the viewer can identify, and to whom extraordinary things happen, or who finds themselves in conflict with an inverted world or who overcomes obstacles. Lewis Carroll's *Alice in Wonderland* (1865) is hugely appealing to animators as it incorporates all of these features. Wonderland offers young Alice a view of her life seen from a very new perspective, full of adults behaving very oddly. As in most fantasies there is a twisted logic – it sort of makes sense, after having seen cats without smiles, to see a smile without a cat. It's this lateral thinking that is so right for animation. Alice is very much a Sunday afternoon full of pondering life's curiosities, but imagine how those favoured elements of drama: a ticking clock, and something huge at stake, might have turned *Alice* into more of a tense, exciting adventure. Does your story have a change of perspective and tension? If not, this may be worth exploring.

▶

Alice in Wonderland 1950

animator
Lou Benin

Alice in Wonderland, with its twisted logic, is much beloved by animators. In addition to the 1950 film shown here, and of course Disney's 1951 version, there is a truly remarkable 1988 adaptation by Jan Švankmajer.

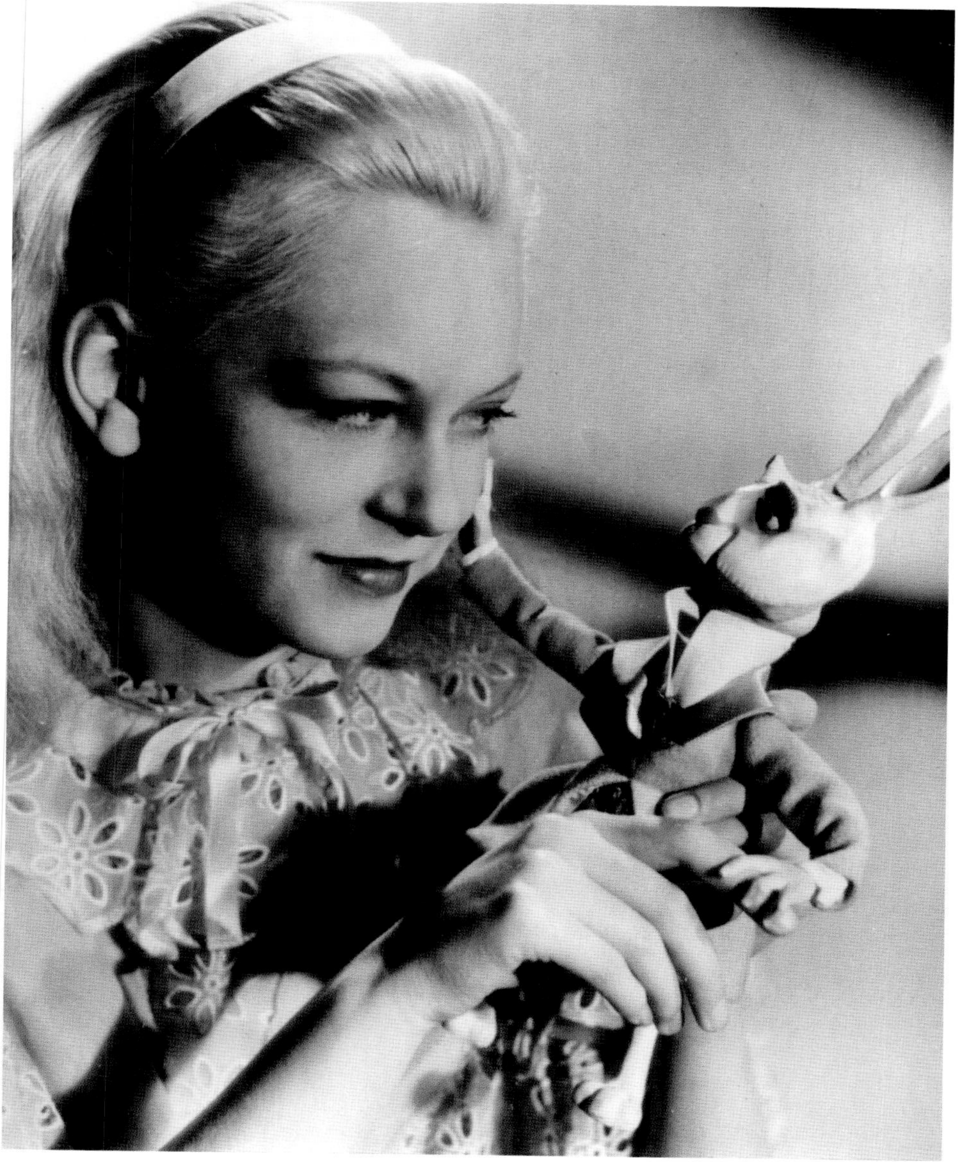

A change of perspective

A change of perspective is often illuminating, as characters such as Charles Dickens' Scrooge painfully realised. For this reason they are always a fruitful place to start a story. A shift in perspective can be dramatised through a conflict between two worlds such as in *Corpse Bride* (2005). In a nice twist, *Enchanted* (2007) used a live-action perspective to show the animated characters what they were missing in their world. Writers and dramatists use this displacement as a device for eventually seeing oneself or one's world clearly. Most such stories begin by setting up a situation that's comfortable, which is then complicated or changed through threats, quests, secrets, revelations, ambition, oppositions, deprivations and achievements. These are then resolved after some sort of journey and confrontation. The more obstacles that are overcome by the main character, the richer the conclusion.

In fantasy worlds, the main characters see what is familiar in a new and different light. Recent films such as *Madame Tutli-Putli* (2007) and *Coraline* (2009), where the reality of the story is very fluid, lend themselves perfectly to stop-motion. *Coraline* particularly has a disturbing world of 'others' – a very twisted variation on the heroine's family. The very physicality of the puppets and sets add credibility to the fantasy. Drawn and CG animation have no boundaries and anything is possible, but stop-motion is grounded by this physicality and the fantasy is stronger where it overcomes these limitations.

Coraline 2009

director
Henry Selick

As Lewis Carroll's Alice falls down a rabbit hole, or steps through a looking glass, so Coraline ventures through a secret opening to discover a very different variation of her world. This secret opening could equally have been a wardrobe or any other of dozens of effective devices.

Focusing the idea

A **fable** is a short story, typically with animals as characters, conveying a moral. It can also be a supernatural story incorporating elements of myth and legend.

An **allegory** is a story, poem or picture that can be interpreted to reveal a hidden meaning, typically a moral or political one.

Fantasy, fable and allegory

A film about a robot stranded on a planet picking up rubbish is certainly about the problems facing such a robot, but at its core *Wall-E* (2008) is much more a story about the human condition, loneliness and the need for a partner. Fish may not conduct clear father-and-son relationships but *Finding Nemo* (2003) was certainly more about that than observations about marine life. Similarly, *Pinocchio* (1940) is less about the inner workings of a puppet than about the dilemma every one of us has faced: that of leaving behind our childhood and facing emotional responsibilities as we grow up.

To some extent, putting well-observed life lessons into the voices of animals, robots or cars can be seen as using 'a spoonful of sugar to help the medicine go down' but it's also about using fantasy, **fable** and **allegory** to show the truth directly and selectively.

Often a visual metaphor is simply stronger and more appealing than the cold hard truth; something Aesop, Hans Andersen and others knew all too well. Imagine how less interesting it would have been had George Orwell not put his politics into the mouths of pigs in *Animal Farm*, or if the four Pevensie children hadn't gone through the wardrobe into the land of Narnia but had instead been straightforwardly told the story of Christ. These metaphors also remove much of the clutter associated with more realistic, complex human characters, while also giving storytellers the opportunity to make witty comparisons. Most fables and fairy tales have animals centre stage. In truth, most have little to do with animals but are using the animal to say something selective about the human condition.

Exercise: Out of this world

Taking a character from one world and transporting them to another, twisted reality is a much-loved trick of authors and animators. Make a list of five of your favourites (for example, *The Wizard of Oz* or Philip Pullman's *His Dark Materials*) and consider how you might make the shift between realities visually or aurally clear. Consider the sudden jump to glorious Technicolor when Dorothy arrives in Oz or Coraline's 'other' parents' button eyes.

How would you achieve the same effect?

Approaching the story > A change of perspective > Out of the mouths of… talking umbrellas?

Getting away with it

Another reason to tell your story through animation or puppetry is that sometimes it can let you say things that a real person cannot. Puppets have a long tradition of verbally attacking great institutions or public figures and getting away with it. Who wants to be seen as being outraged by slander from a puppet? Animated TV series such as *Rick and Steve – The Happiest Gay Couple*, *Life's a Zoo*, *Spitting Image*, and most recently *Headcases* have indulged in gloriously offensive behaviour that live actors might not carry off or which might have repercussions for the actors themselves. However, in addition to the outlandish behaviour there should always be an element of recognisable truth. By hiding behind animated puppets the animator can be more liberated and ultimately more honest and observant. Have a look at Jirí Trnka's poetic but potent *The Hand* (1965) and Jan Švankmajer's *Death of Stalinism in Bohemia* (1990) to see examples of powerful political metaphor.

So if you have found yourself a story about human relations or concerns, would it be liberated by being told using animals or ants or robots? Is it too controversial to have human characters acting it out? Have you found an angle, a perspective, a distancing device, that will allow your story to be truthful?

There has to be a reason for using animation, other than the indulgent joy of being directly responsible for bringing things to life or creating strange environments. Animation has to add something to your film that live action and a few special effects cannot and that 'something different' very often involves a shift of perspective.

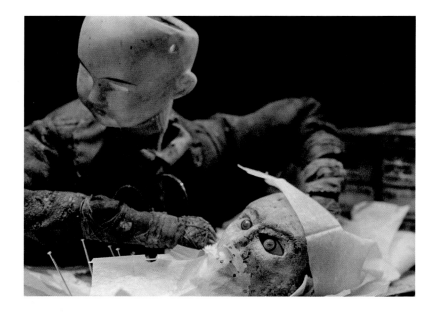

◄

Animal Farm 1954

directors
Halas and Batchelor

Halas and Batchelor's glorious
Animal Farm; anthropomorphism
at its most didactic and
digestible.

The Brothers Quay

Animators such as the Brothers Quay
don't just offer a change of perspective,
they make up their own. Their worlds are
totally unique and bear very little relation
to our world. Their characters often appear
to inhabit a secret world made up of things
we have discarded, or events that seem
to be happening as we have our backs
turned. Theirs is a world that is so
appropriate to stop-motion, relying on
broken objects, often dolls, and textures,
with very real materials being imbued with
some purpose, and all enjoying the quirky
movement of our particular animation
technique. Simple everyday objects such
as a comb take on a huge significance.
This is one of their strengths; they can give
even a screw being tightened in a piece of
wood some tension and drama. Why
shouldn't such objects have their own
stories and meanings and nightmares?

◄

Street of Crocodiles 1986

directors
The Brothers Quay

From broken dolls and
abandoned objects the Brothers
Quay produce disturbing films
unlike any others, often about
broken and abandoned
characters, and full of menace,
where even the smallest
forgotten article is given
unsettling resonances.

A short scene from Disney's *Mary Poppins* (1964) sums up perfectly the point of animation, although ironically this scene is live action. Mary is about to leave the family she has healed. She's clearly a bit tearful and agrees politely with her talking parrot umbrella that perhaps the family could have been more grateful. The parrot is about to launch into an honest tirade against the family but Mary quietly clamps its mouth shut – she doesn't really need to hear a truth that she knows already but can't speak. Surely the point of animation is to say things, or to point out ideas, that can't be expressed in our everyday lives?

Ciphers

As always, Shakespeare got there first, with the use of the 'play within a play' device in *Hamlet*. Hamlet stages a very artificial play containing a heightened version of a murder. It bears only a passing likeness to the murder of the King, but the essential truth is there for Claudius, the murderer, to confront all too plainly. So often, like Mary's parrot, drama needs a device or character, and often a very private one, that lets the main character externalise their thoughts. In animation, Jiminy Cricket in *Pinocchio* (1940) is a prime example and, at the other extreme, there's a gloriously irreverent film, *Marquis* (1989), where the live actors have animal masks, and the Marquis de Sade, imprisoned in the Bastille, has an **animatronic** talking penis that acts as his conscience. Similarly, the great play, *Harvey*, gives the main character not only alcohol as a way of speaking the truth, but also gives him an invisible six-foot tall rabbit to talk to. A suggestion of mental unbalance allows an extra degree of speaking what is normally unspoken. Similarly, the superhero persona is usually more honest than the repressed civilian, just as Mr Hyde was the true character behind Dr Jekyll. There are so many ways to change the perspective to see the truth.

Focusing the idea

Ciphers tend to be minor characters who carry out the will or bidding of a more dominant character.

Animatronics is the technique of making and operating characters, performed through various hidden levers and cables, as real-time lifelike models (see page 93) that can interact with live-action actors.

▲

Mary Poppins 1964

director
Robert Stevenson

Mary Poppins and her perceptive umbrella, saying all the things she can't express herself. The visiting mysterious outsider who causes a family to see themselves afresh is a great narrative device, and can be seen in classics such as *The Nutcracker* and *Peter Pan*.

Speaking honestly

Has the main character in your film got an interesting way of revealing his inner thoughts quite naturally, rather than just saying what he feels? Try to structure your story so that it contains a device that allows the characters to see their dilemmas clearly, or to speak their thoughts honestly. This can be anything from a change of technique, or narrative convention, to an imaginary companion. Also, for us as storytellers, it's so much easier to talk honestly through a third person, or from behind a mask, and animation (particularly puppets) fulfils the role of a third person beautifully.

Balance 1989

directors
Christoph and
Wolfgang Lauenstein

A film that finds a succinct visual metaphor for a very human dilemma. Here characters find themselves on a suspended slab and their existence depends on cooperation and trust. Animation is particularly suitable for these metaphors.

Recommended viewing

Balance (1989) is a fantastic example of the strength of metaphor in animation. It records the plight of five characters who live on a floating slab in the middle of a void. They all move in synch with each other in order to keep the platform balanced. However, this harmony is disrupted when one character drags a box onto the platform, which everyone wants to investigate. The resultant movements unbalance the platform and all but one character is either pushed or falls into space. The final character is left precariously balanced with the box out of reach.

We don't need to know who the characters are nor how they got there, let alone how the great slab is suspended – but the image is a great metaphor of mistrust and cooperation. Some writers might pen several volumes to express the futility and frustration experienced in a few minutes by these characters. A picture is indeed worth a thousand words.

Focusing the idea

Animated films are often described as having a dreamlike or nightmarish quality. This effect can be the result of jumbling up familiar events into surreal contexts, where unconnected concerns and events start to have terrifying or joyous links, and where, literally, anything can happen. In addition to the dreamlike feeling they can produce, dream sequences have been a standby part of even the earliest stop-motion films such as Edwin Porter's *Dream of a Rarebit Fiend* (1906) and the films of Georges Méliès. They allow the narrative to showcase animation and special effects and other such tricks.

Dreams and nightmares

Dreams are a convention beloved of writers and dramatists because they permit information to be conveyed to the audience, or to reveal a character's inner thoughts, their hopes, or a back-story. This has been such a popular device that it is now seen as a rather lazy and too-convenient option. For this reason, dream scenarios work best when the protagonist is unaware of being in a dream or where there is an element of doubt as to what is real and what is not. There are many films based on the idea of a dream, but they are usually little more than an excuse for a series of imaginative images. In the real world, even the flimsiest of dreams starts with some thought or theme; they illuminate familiar subjects with a new light. A dream narrative, then, works best when given some logic, however twisted, and some perspective, rather than being the justification for some striking but unconnected visuals.

Skhizein 2008

director
Jérémy Clapin for
Dark Prince

The disturbing and melancholic
Skhizein; its themes of mental
dislocation are given a visual
metaphor by the character
literally existing many
centimetres from himself as
a result of contact with a
meteorite. It is made more
disturbing by its delicate and
beautiful art direction.

Exercise: Dreams

Have a look at how dreams have been
used in films, plays and literature, and see
if you feel cheated by the fact that it was
all a dream, or whether some element of
the character or plot has been illuminated.
Try to remember one of your own recent
dreams and structure it into a short
scenario that says something about your
own experience or emotions that day,
making the most of the change of
perspective. Do you see the dream as
your fears or your hopes exposed? Is the
dream saying something you can't?

Not just for kids

The idea of cartoons or puppets tackling very serious and mature themes or documentary subjects can initially seem odd, as we are conditioned to thinking of animation as something for children. However, looking at the history of animation, most subjects and nearly all genres have been tackled.

Sometimes the self-conscious tricks of animation do get in the way, and you can watch the showy animation without connecting to the subject. On other occasions the animation can be seen to trivialise an important subject. However, one of the strengths of animation, its allegorical nature, is to let us see things free of stereotype, free of clutter and free of blinkers. The Leonard Cheshire Disability charity and Aardman Animations created a series of commercials called *Creature Discomforts* that feature animals sculpted in the familiar *Creature Comforts* style, but each of which has physical and/or sensory impairments. It works not by using humorous animation to sugar-coat a difficult subject, dislocating it from reality, but by challenging our perceptions of disability from a very fresh, accessible visual angle. Leonard Cheshire Disability worked closely with Aardman, on both the audio interviews with disabled people and the characters, to ensure the representations of disability were just right.

It was worth the effort as the selectiveness of the animation process allows metaphorical aspects of the characters' stories to become clear, helping the audience to connect with them on a more direct level.

Similarly, there have been at least three animated versions of *The Diary of Anne Frank*, all technically excellent, and sensitive. With the story based on such real and vivid tragedy, they have been uncomfortable experiences. This may be because the literal approaches to the animation seem inadequate to convey such complex emotions. It is hard to even begin to conceive a puppet version of Anne Frank, although we should avoid the idea that there are some subjects that we have to shy away from. But if you are going to tackle a topic as sensitive as this then be sure you are using the most appropriate approach. Such serious themes often work best when treated through metaphor and heavy styling.

Creature Discomforts 2008

animator
Aardman

Allegories can work just as well with serious subjects as for trivial ones. And a puppet, especially with its connections with sculpture, effigies, dolls, tombs and such, is an object that comes with the potential of allegory built in. Stop-motion can use this to its advantage.

Focusing the idea

When developing your story it is important to consider the logistics it will require. The economics of stop-motion and of building puppets mean that it is rarely practical to structure a script around dozens of characters that only appear briefly on screen. Once you have gone to all the trouble of building a puppet you might as well make the most of it. He or she exists and that's one of the major expenses covered. If you have a puppet it makes very little difference, other than general wear and tear to the puppet, whether the character has to carry a short film or a feature. This is in stark contrast to a drawn film or a clay film where the character has to be redrawn and resculpted for every scene.

So much effort and expense goes into the making of puppets that it's best to concentrate on fewer characters. This of course tightens a narrative and you might have to be ingenious in finding ways to convey what might otherwise have been delivered by incidental characters or crowds. The Wallace and Gromit half-hour specials, for example, have few secondary characters, but with clever storytelling and strong relationships the world of West Wallaby Street doesn't look under-populated.

Crowds

For CG films there are a range of programs to replicate characters into vast crowds, each slightly different in look and behaviour. It is, of course, very different in stop-motion where featuring dozens of different characters, apart from being dramatically suspect, would be impractical.

That said, however, crowd scenes are not impossible in stop-motion. There are various optical and staging tricks to help, but in shooting a crowd scene you are going to get only a few seconds of animation shot in a day. I once shot a commercial involving 32 Viennese Whirls, complete with sashes and gloves, dancing Strauss' *Emperor Waltz* in a ballroom. Thanks to a well-placed mirror and some devious choreography, we managed to raise that number considerably – a trick used very early in Starewicz's films. Of course, computer graphics and blue screens would help today.

▲

Babylon 1986

directors
Peter Lord and
David Sproxton

A still from the early Aardman
film, *Babylon*, featuring dozens
of immaculately dressed
characters. Happily, most of
them were sitting down.
A true epic.

Making a little go a long way

A stop-motion film full of characters walking and running is going to be much more complex and time consuming to shoot than a film full of talking heads. So when you're planning your film do think about what you really need to show on screen and what you can simply imply. A recent beautiful film, *Gargoyle* (2008) by Michael Cusack, manages to tell a haunting story with just two characters. It is satisfying to spend so much time with such well-crafted characters.

My own films have concentrated on just a few characters, and any necessary crowd puppets and secondary characters have been less sophisticated puppets. Another tactic is to give your 'extras' interchangeable elements to make them go further. For example, the courtiers in an early scene in *Rigoletto* (1993) appeared a short while later redressed and dirtied up as beggars.

The level of expression required for your character and how literal the lip synch needs to be both add to the expense of your puppet. If you are happy with limited movement in the faces, it will save considerably on the budget but put more pressure on the body language. This in turn affects the storytelling. It is essential to have in mind a clear idea of just how the narrative will be told before designing the characters. If the film is told mainly in wide shots, costly facial mechanics would be redundant. If the character is confined to a chair, does it really need articulated legs? If you're thinking that at some point it might walk then make sure you make that decision during the storyboard stage of pre-production. It's an odd way to budget films, but certain activities and gestures are more expensive than others and this must be taken into account.

Exercise: Essentials

Take a well-known story, film or play and see how far you can pare down the number of characters and locations, and find devices that might impart plot and information otherwise done by characters. You can turn this reduction into something creative. Again, it is all about not being literal. Most animation is about telling the biggest stories with only the most essential elements.

Focusing the idea

▲

Gargoyle 2008

animator
Michael Cusack

It will never hurt the narrative to
focus on just a few characters.
This is the complete cast from
Michael Cusack's film *Gargoyle*.

Atmosphere and substance > Economics

Keep out of the water

Animation can certainly do most things, but you'd be giving yourself unnecessary headaches by making a film where most of the stop-motion characters spend their time indulging in such activities as swimming or flying. The sheer practicalities of this, while an exciting and possibly rewarding challenge, would surely lead a producer to consider other techniques. The need for so much water in the plot prompted Aardman's *Flushed Away* (2006) to be achieved through CG animation. It's recognised that this was not necessarily a satisfactory result as their characters lost what makes them so endearing. A film such as *Finding Nemo* (2003) would have been extraordinarily difficult with stop-motion – especially the translucent jellyfish. On the other hand, a film like *Cars* (2006) might have worked well in stop-motion, depending on how flexible the cars were, though the essence of speed would have been hard to capture without blurring.

The point is that you must consider the technical, practical aspects of your puppets when approaching a story. Fluffy, floaty, smoky, wispy, transparent, wet; all would be cause for grief if treated through stop-motion. None of them is impossible, but puppets have an undeniable physical presence that is best exploited. This is their strength; make use of it.

▲

There There 2003

director
Chris Hopewell

This music video for Radiohead's song *There There*, by Chris Hopewell of Collision Films, not only features large numbers of stop-motion characters, but is mixed with live action and shot on a tight budget. Quite a feat.

Fur

Animation and animals go hand in hand, or paw in paw. But if you are using stop-motion for a story with furry characters then you had better be prepared to accept a certain amount of crawling (movement and twitching in the fur caused by the animator's constant touching of the puppets), although that didn't take anything away from King Kong. The only alternative is to spend a huge amount of expensive, inventive work in the manufacture of the puppets to avoid the crawling. The puppets in *Fantastic Mr Fox* (2009) do have fur but they have been designed in such a way as to reduce crawling to a minimum. Sometimes, puppets' fur has been sculpted as part of the latex or silicon skin, with a few strands of hair to confuse the issue. Another approach is to make the fur very stylised. Again, there is no getting away from the fact that puppets are touched, and with textures such as fur and cloth, this can be a problem. Likewise long hair drawn onto a character in the design stage looks beautiful, but the practicalities are another matter. If you don't animate it, it looks unnatural and lifeless. If you do, an awful amount of time will be taken up by hair alone. Can you create an equally interesting design look but without the long hair? As always, it is a balance between the creative and the practical.

It is important to think carefully about exactly what will be required of the puppets. For example, the furry characters in *Monsters Inc* (2001), especially Sully, would have been impossible in stop-motion, and I suspect this is a challenge that excited the CG animators for that very reason.

Essentially, in film-making the practicalities and economics cannot be separated from the storytelling, most especially with stop-motion where everything has to be built, and there's less chance of reusing material.

Tip: Intimacy versus panoramic views

Stop-motion, with its table-top sets, is able to suggest intimate locations very well through the use of close-ups and mid-shots. However, restricted budgets can often prevent the use of huge wide panoramas and vistas, as these, traditionally, have to be built and take up considerable, expensive space. Sometimes, such as when I directed *Hamilton Mattress* (2001), good old theatrical tricks of false perspective create the illusion of space and scale, but now most stop-motion sets are supplemented through CG and blue-screen work, allowing for more scale.

Atmosphere and substance > Economics

In Chapter 3 we'll find out what qualities a puppet can bring to a film that actors, drawn and computer-generated images cannot. We'll look at why stop-motion puppets have an extra element of life and spontaneity about them. We'll also look at how to get the most out of a puppet in design terms. In particular we'll focus on exploiting the features of a puppet, such as the eyes and the hands, that are best for expression, and how to make them as easy to animate as possible.

Finally, we will also discuss other techniques that involve physically touching and manipulating objects under camera to tell a story. These techniques clearly demonstrate that a complicated puppet is not always necessary to tell an affecting story.

◀

Rigoletto 1993

animator
Barry Purves

My *Rigoletto* puppet made by Mackinnon and Saunders is a great example of a very expressive face. Mackinnon and Saunders are UK-based stop-motion puppet makers, sculptors and artists. Their characters have made many an animator's life easier – knowing the puppet will perform, the animator can concentrate on the animation.

Focusing the idea > **The puppets** > Preparations

Puppets, in all their many forms, can't even begin to accurately reproduce the complex and multi-faceted, idiosyncratic and random movement of live action. Nor can they have the precise fluidity of CG or the freedom of drawn animation – nor should they. As we've already seen, they have their own very distinct qualities; they exist and their performance is intrinsically tied up with how they are operated. They have credibility, a tangible presence and a physical distinctiveness that even the most casual, disconnected viewer is aware of. This is one of the particular motivations for telling an animated story with puppets and objects.

The fact that big emotions, drama, tension and humour can all be conveyed through what are clearly pieces of brass, wood, fabric, silicon and clay is part of the appeal of puppets and stop-motion. They are credible because they exist as part of a physical world. The effect is not realistic, but the physicality of the puppets gives their actions credibility, and an immediate connection with the audience. Because the viewer can see the puppets existing in a real space, reacting to lights, focus, gravity and to each other, it makes their performance more believable.

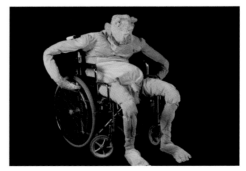

Simple puppets

Complex puppets are not essential for telling a story, and many animators enjoy getting as much storytelling as possible out of very simple materials. Sometimes animators don't use puppets at all but just objects or even materials such as sand and salt, and when that works the results can be sublime. Creating beautiful, resonant imagery and movement out of something as simple as sand requires inventive technique and a detailed understanding of light, movement, shade and texture. It also requires an equally imaginative approach to storytelling. Getting so much out of so little is enormously satisfying.

Working with figurative characters such as puppets may perhaps seem an advantage, but even so the puppet has to be designed to maximise its potential for expression. Some puppets are so elaborate that their constant movement can become counter-productive, and what is being expressed can easily be lost. These overly complex puppets sometimes resolutely refuse to spring into life. Conversely there are puppets that are little more than a block of wood, but a well-timed tilt or attitude suggests an immediately recognisable scenario. The secret is in enjoying the puppet, making everything count, and only having what is necessary. These are some of the strengths of stop-motion.

Infinite variety

Four very different types of puppet, whose techniques directly affect how the puppets move and thus what is possible in the narrative. From the top we see: Ronnie Burkett's complex marionettes; the inventive ultra-violet puppets of Purves Puppets; a character from Michelangelo Fornaro's *Lo Guarracino* (2004) and the full-scale pixilated Rex from *Reg's Revenge* by Nat Miller. What one method would find easy, another would find impossible.

All my Relations 1990

animator
Joanna Priestley

This image was created with dog food, among other materials, and demonstrates that expensive, complicated puppets aren't always necessary.

Telling the story with puppets > The physical puppet

The physical puppet

The unavoidable truth about any stop-motion puppet or animated object is that the animator is going to have to touch it for every single frame. This is one of the most appealing aspects of the process to many animators. To maintain the necessary poses a puppet usually requires an interior skeleton with a robust durability that can also be easily controlled. When designing a puppet you must think of how and where it will be held. Usually, any animation is going to need two hands; probably with your left hand stabilising and gripping the puppet very tightly, whilst the right hand, acting with leverage, moves the elements necessary for that frame without disturbing anything else. Every puppet needs a solid place to grip firmly, and in figurative puppets this usually ends up being in the chest area. A block of balsa or a solid framework in the chest is ideal. Using something such as foam would compress as you gripped the puppet, and may not always spring back to the right place, causing unwelcome twitching. Likewise any fancy piece of costume, such as frills, placed where you will hold the puppet can only get in the way.

▲

Corpse Bride 2005

director
Tim Burton and
Mike Johnson

Mike Johnson posing with the key characters from *Corpse Bride*. The bride's veil had tiny wires stitched into the lace to allow the animation to appear fluid, but there were still some shots where the veil was computer generated.

Armatures

The material used to construct the skeletons and armatures within the puppet will depend largely on the budget you have available. A cheap option is to make a skeleton from simple aluminium wire. Unfortunately these have very limited durability as, once bent, they simply cannot be straightened again. Also, as you bend the wire into a desired shape it may bend elsewhere – causing all sorts of problems with continuity. This can be controlled to some extent by wrapping balsa around the parts you don't want to move. Using soft-tempered aluminium wire (which can be bent easily and has little spring back) will also help. But wire is still far from ideal. So, the aluminium wire approach is fine for background puppets where limited and less subtle movement is required, but for main characters armatures are pretty essential. It's an expense that will be well worth it.

Even a very basic armature will help you produce nicely controlled animation. Generally, armatures are a series of ball-and-socket joints linked by stiff rods, which allow flexibility while also giving clean and maintained definition to the limbs. An armature should be capable of free and subtle movement, without disturbing anything else, and yet should also be rock steady so as not to droop when the animator moves away. This contradiction makes it clear that building an armatured skeleton is a complex art, and that the tensioning of a puppet can make or break the animation. It is therefore very important to work closely with the puppet makers and get as much experience as possible dealing with different kinds of armature.

The number of joints, and therefore to some extent the expense of the armature, depends on exactly what you want from your puppet. For example, there's little point in building a multi-jointed spine if all the character does is lie in bed. Go through your script and see exactly what is required of your puppet, and if you can afford an armature, then go for it. One decent puppet is certainly better than several wobbly ones. Once again, structure your film around what you know is achievable with your resources and budget.

There's just something visceral about moving a puppet frame by frame.... There's a magical quality about it. Maybe you can get smoother animation with computers, but there's a dimension and emotional quality to this kind of animation that fits these characters and this story [*Corpse Bride*].

Tim Burton

Telling the story with puppets > **The physical puppet** > Telling characteristics

Heads

Stop-motion puppets with animatable faces usually rely on an internal skull with a complex arrangement of levers and paddles attached to an outer skin. This can produce a huge variety of expressions, with the advantage that you can have a large increment one frame and a small one the next. Obviously such mechanics are expensive (unless you have the skills to make them yourself), and add to the weight of the puppet. They can also sometimes make the puppets top heavy. Some of the levers can be manipulated simply by fingers or shaped lollipop sticks, and you have to trust that the lever will stay in place. Elements where the movement might fight the natural tension of the skin, such as an opening jaw, might need a geared device to hold it open.

Detailed, complex faces are fine if you can afford them, and have the time available to animate them, but don't always assume that a complex face is necessary to tell a story. Economy can lead to creative results and a good body-led performance from the puppet can often convey more than literal facial expressions. Look at your film and ask how important facial expressions are, and whether there is a more interesting way to communicate.

▶

In the Fall of Gravity 2008

animator
Ron Cole

Here we see Trevor and his highly complex head armature from Ron Cole's extraordinary *In the Fall of Gravity*. If you have the budget for a sophisticated armature it is well worth the investment.

Below

Unlike drawn or CG animation, in stop-motion when a puppet character lifts a foot it will fall over, and when you are animating it, it will slide around. For this reason, every puppet has to be firmly anchored to the set. Various techniques can help here. For example, lightweight puppets can be pinned through the feet to a soft board, although this will affect the design of the sets.

Another technique is to have metal plates on the feet and a perforated steel set, under which strong magnets are located and moved about as appropriate. These magnets aren't cheap, and can affect any nearby computers. They can also damage your hands as they snap together, but they are strong and they last; they can allow a puppet to stand on one foot, as long as the joints are suitably tensioned. However, the need for perforated steel will clearly affect the design of the set and this may not work for the look of your film. These perforations in the steel are essential, not only for focusing the magnetism, but they also allow you to poke pins through for guidance.

However, magnets may be difficult if your character has small feet or delicate paws. An alternative technique is to secure the feet with tie-downs; these are lockable devices that screw through from under the set into the foot. This has the advantage of totally gripping the foot tightly, giving a strong visual impression of the puppet connecting to its environment. However, it is a very fiddly process and requires easy access for the animator as well as a great deal of planning as it is necessary to pre-drill the holes in the set. It's also very easy to dislodge the puppet while you are manipulating it.

Another much cheaper technique, which has been used in many films, is to cut down the walking by letting the camera do much of the movement, or to put the characters in vehicles, getting a lot of easy action.

▶

Screen Play 1992

animator
Barry Purves

Because of limited access under the set, the feet of the puppets in *Screen Play* contained small magnets to secure them. This was not ideal as it is hard to lift a foot a little off the ground. Removable magnets under the set are more practical.

Outside

Clothes over a puppet can remove the need for complex sculpting of a body as long as they are well tailored around basic shapes attached to the skeleton. These solid shapes, usually balsa or resin, help keep the silhouette of the character clear and consistent even after much animation.

Also, with costumed puppets, there's not much skin on display so you can often limit this to hands and faces. If you need to have a naked or partially naked character then remember that exposed flesh will get dirty and then need to be replaced, which can be very expensive. The all over 'skin' will also make the puppet heavier, as well as making the seam lines from the moulding process more difficult to hide.

Rigoletto 1993

animator
Barry Purves

Here we see Gilda, inside and out, as created by Mackinnon and Saunders. The clothing should be well tailored to the puppet to prevent unnecessary movement from repeated touching, but must not be restrictive.

Jack the Giant Killer 1962

director
Nathan Juran

Unclothed characters make life harder for the model makers.

The puppets

 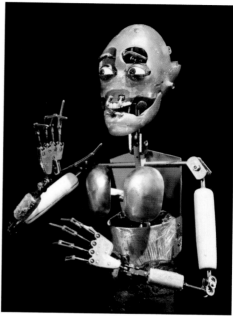

Tip: Skin

The skin you select for your puppet will depend on the available budget as well as the requirements of the animation. Latex can be baked over the armature in a mould and painted as necessary. It has a lovely flesh-like quality; stretching and wrinkling easily. However, it has a limited life, tending to become 'crunchy' after a while – and it gets dirty very easily.

Silicon is also a good option as it has a more translucent feel, appropriate to skin, lasts longer than latex and is also easier to clean. On the other hand, it lacks the flexibility of latex and is much heavier. A combination of silicon and latex can also be used, giving the best of each material. Plasticine faces are a practical and economic alternative, but what you save in construction you will spend in resculpting time, and some detail will be necessarily sacrificed. Of course there is no definitive way of creating skin. This being animation, you could use any material: newspaper print, leather, silk... anything appropriate to

In stop-motion animation we often don't have the luxury of time. It is therefore helpful if your characters are designed to reveal their core characteristics visually and immediately. This is especially true for short films, which need to make the most of every frame, telling the audience as much as possible, as economically as possible. The puppet's appearance can be the audience's first clue to its character and history. To help this process, many designers think of their characters in terms of shapes and silhouettes, and what this says about the character. For example, it may be hard to imbue a very sharp pointy angular character with much warmth, and conversely a more rounded, wobbly character might find it hard to portray evil. Softness and curves are inevitably associated with cute and cuddly, as are big saucer eyes.

So much can be conveyed from the way a character looks, but animators must also think about how the character will move, and how the moving elements of the design can be used expressively. For example, think how a tail might be used to show a particular emotion, or whether there are shoulders that can be shrugged. The perfect expression comes when design and movement work together. A haughty character will often be tall, looking down on everyone else, and they will probably walk in a clipped, controlled manner. Conversely a 'goofy' character will be flexible, and saggy, almost boneless and uncoordinated. It's easy to dismiss these elements of design as stereotyping, but when you have limited time to tell your story they can be an invaluable visual shorthand.

▲

The Family Story 2009

animator
Chris Walsh

Here we have a charming example of pushing and exaggerating human proportions to make characters less literal.

The puppets

Expressiveness

It's essential when writing and storyboarding your film to think how the characters will express themselves. Will they rely on dialogue to reveal their thoughts, or will they speak to the audience through highly complex facial expressions or lively body language?

Whatever the answer, it will affect the design of the puppet and the storytelling of the film itself. If facial expressions and dialogue are important, you will want to show them in a range of close-ups. In this case you must ensure that your puppet will stand up under the scrutiny of a close-up, where every detail is revealed. For example the eyes must be alive enough, and focused so that the viewer can read them in close-up.

Conversely, if you don't want to tell your story through facial expressions, then a reliance on body language will suggest plenty of wide shots, giving a very different feel to the film. Remember that wide shots take longer to film, as there's considerably more to animate. All this, of course, affects the budget. When designing a puppet you need to make sure it is equipped to express what you want and how you want it. Does your puppet have a decent enough skeleton to use its body to act out emotions? Does it have long enough legs to provide those elegant strides you want? Students often draw beautiful storyboards with the characters going through all manner of physical contortions. The reality of the physical puppet is often less dynamic.

Ami 2008

animator
Dominique Bongers

You don't need a complex puppet to tell an affecting story. Here strong design, clear body language and a remarkable use of coffee granules create a beautiful and delicate graphic effect appropriate to the story. A charming use of a cheap material that can even be recycled!

Spatial awareness

An economic design will only work if every piece of the design is telling some part of the same story. If your cast consists of a family of eggs, or billiard balls, or footballs, you're going to fight to make any movement and design interesting. The shapes made by a billiard ball moving through space are not going to register at all unless there is sufficient detail, such as a face, on the ball. It is important to enjoy the movement of your characters, and an egg looks much the same whichever way it faces. It is therefore necessary to find interesting shapes that read from every angle, and that change as a character moves. An egg spinning won't work until it is given arms, for example, and then the slightest move will register. It's always worth imagining your characters in silhouette and whether they still read.

A Traditional Christmas at Small Birds Singing 2009

director
Linda McCarthy

The ceramic heads of these puppets force the acting to come from the movement of the heads and bodies rather than facial expressions.

The puppets

Anatomy

The way in which the characters move in a spatial setting is crucial to any stop-motion film. For example, if you give your potentially elegant character short legs, it will dictate a rather comedic walk. If you give your character huge legs, a stride will take him across the set in a few frames, quicker than the other characters. Big fat chunky feet will necessitate lifting the knees higher than usual to allow for the feet to be flicked through. This may be just the effect you're looking for, but remember that every small detail on the puppet will have some bearing on its movement, and can be a further means of expression.

If your character is a dog but you have made it walk on two legs, this will affect how the head and especially the eyes either side of the snout will move. Sometimes the anatomy of snouts and beaks prevent the audience from seeing both eyes at the same time, except from the front. This will limit the movement of the head, or necessitate a very flexible neck. Mouths that are not usually used for talking may have to be moved around a face to be seen, or else the head might need to be held in an unnatural position. Look all around you and see just how people's anatomy affects how they move and react. With drawn animation, CG and clay the animators can slightly cheat and give the characters a rather fluid anatomy. Puppets are more solid, having to obey their rigid mechanics, which is part of their charm and credibility, but may also be a drawback. Make sure that when you are designing a puppet, all the features work in practical terms. Will the camera see everything, and will the anatomy hinder the animation?

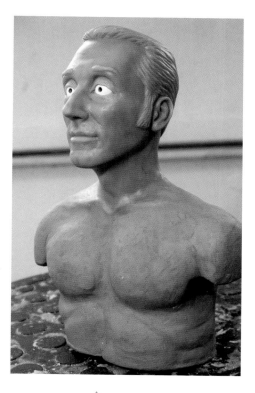

▲

Friendly Fire 2008

director
Andy Kaiser

As can be seen in this initial sculpt for a soldier in *Friendly Fire*, most puppets begin their three-dimensional life as clay models. These can be sculpted until the features are perfected at which stage a latex or silicon mould is taken.

Stylised movement

Unlike in the very early days of film-making, when there were few alternatives, there's little point now in using a puppet to do what a human actor or CG character can do perfectly well. Digital visual effects can now place actors in scenes that danger or sheer impracticality wouldn't otherwise allow. CG can even take an actor, and through motion capture and CG design transform his features into a fantasy creature, as happened with Andy Serkis and Gollum and in Peter Jackson's *King Kong* (2005). It is a CG creation, but with a very slick, believable movement and nuanced performance still based on the original actor. A puppet, though, will always look like a puppet and it seems perverse not to enjoy the way it looks and moves.

Another obvious advantage of using puppets is that they do not have the baggage that some actors, especially famous actors, bring with them. Actors are billed by their real names at the head of the film, so you know they are playing a part, and it usually takes an audience a little while to get past that. With stop-motion, even though the audience has the double knowledge that they are watching puppets portraying characters, they can still plunge straight into the story. Audiences can connect with puppets immediately without thinking about the actors' previous films or their celebrity lifestyles.

▶

The Dark Crystal 1982

directors
Jim Henson and **Frank Oz**

Puppets don't have the physical limitations of actors, and can therefore easily appear to have unlimited stamina. For this reason, it can be very effective to give them a believable physical life by creating the illusion of effort and fatigue. This is beautifully illustrated by the drooping bodies and shuffling steps of the live-action, animatronic Mystics puppets from *The Dark Crystal*.

The puppets

Facial expression

While a puppet can be subtle it will never have the complex details of live action or CG, but that's not what puppets are about. Puppets are about selective representation. A human face has a multitude of muscles all working together to be expressive, letting the skin stretch, wrinkle and contort. Even the best puppet makers could not duplicate those mechanics and their combinations, and that may not be a bad thing. Puppets work by emphasising those elements that define the character, and discarding those that have no storytelling value.

In the recent short film *Friendly Fire* (2008), set in the trenches of World War I, the main characters alternate between live action and animated versions from scene to scene, giving a very fluid and disturbing feel. The film also uses projections of live-action faces on to the puppets, and graphics on the live-action faces help blur the line between the two techniques. The film-makers use this blurring to perfectly echo the nightmarish quality of the scenario. It is a remarkable effect, perfect for the film. (However, the mind boggles at the precision of lining up a projector onto the face of a small, moving puppet.) The effect could have been achieved through CG but it may have been too precise, losing the visceral human element.

On occasion a puppet is of a small scale, limiting the possibility of facial mechanics. A larger, more expressive head can be built for close-ups, but then this does usually require extra bits of set to match, or the use of blue screen. The 1933 King Kong had a full-scale life-size head for certain live-action close-ups and, as it turns out, these were less expressive.

Friendly Fire 2008

director
Andy Kaiser

Here we see a puppet with a human actor's face projected on to it. This effect required a complex rig to project the footage accurately and ensure the puppet was very firmly held in place.

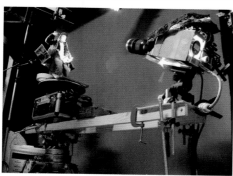

Recommended viewing

It's a Bird (1930) directed by Harold L. Muller, is a highly ingenious short film that includes a stop-motion bird eating its way through the contents of a scrapyard. The bird then lays an egg, which hatches and grows into a full-scale car. All this is achieved complete with camera moves and a live-action character watching. The same story could now be shown relatively easily with CG, but knowing the patience, concentration and memory required to place the items with such accuracy makes it just a little more captivating.

Telling characteristics > **Stylised movement** > Replacements

Being expressive

Live actors can pull as many weird and wonderful facial expressions as they like without adding to the cost of the production. Sadly, the same cannot be said of stop-motion; it's a peculiarity of this medium that expressions add to the budget. This is simply because they take longer to animate. Therefore, if expressions are an important part of your story, you must think carefully about how these will be achieved.

If your film relies on very complex, detailed expressions CG may be a better solution, but this does depend on how literal you want to be. Several well-known stop-motion television series have recently been turned into CG series, and this is often said to be because CG can provide more facial expressions. This is true but a good animator can get a huge amount of expression, feeling and character out of a relatively blank face (especially when it is used in conjunction with effective body language). The lack of complicated facial expression is rarely a hindrance to good acting, especially if the puppet has a versatile body and emotive eyes.

An interesting merger of CG and stop-motion seen in several recent TV series, such as *Postman Pat*, uses featureless puppets on set. The facial expressions are then added by the CG department afterwards, from a library of stock expressions. This is useful if you are hoping to use the same piece of footage for different scenes, but it's harder for the animator with a dead puppet in their hand. However, there are some situations where expressions on the real puppet are paramount. For example, in *Rigoletto* (1993) it would have been absurd not to have used expressive faces because the story demanded a great deal of dynamic singing. Bear in mind, though, that focusing on the faces hinders much movement with the body. To go in for close-ups you must make sure that the dialogue and emotion is an essential part of the piece.

The Astronomer's Sun 2010

director
Jessica Cope

Sometimes facial expressions and body language have such clarity that dialogue becomes redundant. Stop-motion is particularly good at exploiting this idea.

Life's a Zoo 2008–present

creators
Adam Shaheen and
Andrew Horne II

Here we see Morreski, and friend, from *Life's a Zoo*. This series uses vividly realised characters to satirise reality shows and highlight many racial stereotypes.

Recommended viewing

Look at the controlled but expressive physicality of Buster Keaton and the other silent comedians, to see just how much can be expressed through a static face but mobile body. For example, watch the final scene of Keaton's *One Week* (1920) to see emotions from desperation to disappointment to love – all expressed without a word.

Telling characteristics > Stylised movement > Replacements

Replacements

A favourite technique in stop-motion is to use replacements – literally replacing a fixed puppet, or maybe just elements of a face, with a completely new piece, and thus suggesting a move. Replaceable heads can produce different facial expressions without having costly or complex internal mechanics. They do, however, require a great deal of planning during the storyboard stage as you need to know in advance exactly what will be needed and when. You also need to decide exactly when you need to change the heads. Of course, they can be changed in-between shots, but if you want the change to be in full view then you must be able to reach the puppet easily and ensure that the change is not too drastic.

Replacements require perfectly matching paint jobs, accurate alignment and **registration**. Remember that more heads means more available expressions but it also means a bigger budget. It is often hard to find the right combination of replacements to produce a subtle performance – but not all stories require subtlety. For example, replacements are particularly efficient when an action has to be endlessly repeated, such as with marching toy soldiers. In this instance, it might work to have the whole body of such a toy soldier as a series of replacements but with an animatable head moving independently, so that the viewer will not notice the repetition.

Replacements require a certain degree of stylisation to work, and for this reason many animators prefer the flexibility and spontaneity that fully articulated faces offer. These let you choose between a large move and small move exactly at the moment you are animating. With replacements, to some extent, that choice is made for you. However, replacements have recently been used brilliantly in series such as *Pingu*, where the whole puppet was often a replacement.

Registration is the technique by which you ensure that the current shot lines up in every detail with the previous shot. In all forms of animation, it helps to refer back to previous images and any registration, whether it is pegs, charts or gauges, will help make sure the characters are orientated and that all the details line up.

Speed and economics

In addition to being useful for repetitious walk cycles, replacements can also be used for stretching faces to extremes that mechanics can't provide or other effects such as a falling ball bouncing and changing briefly into a flattened shape. Replacements are certainly a much more practical and economical solution than building a ball with complex mechanics. The results can be glorious, but you should consider the planning involved, and the finesse needed so as not to show the difference between the sequential pieces.

My first encounter with replacements was on *Chorlton and the Wheelies* (1976–1979), a series designed to be produced quickly but effectively. Most of the characters were faces on wheels, making them easy to animate.

There was little walking in the show and it was decided that Fenella, the wicked witch, would not walk either. Instead she disappeared into the ground in a series of replacements and then reappeared elsewhere – the restricted budget of the show produced a suitably creative and fortuitously lively solution and one that fits the character and the pacing of the show.

These were pretty basic replacements and Fenella was limited to always disappearing in the same pose, but it was effective. In the same programme, the Wheelies' faces were replaceable with different and somewhat random expressions. There was no sense of moving from one expression to another, they simply changed, but it worked. Remember that necessity is the mother of invention and constraints of time and money can often lead to creative inspiration.

Pingu 1986–2005

Studio
Hit Entertainment

Here we see the gloriously naughty Pingu and his family. Practically all of the animation was achieved through replacements.

George Pál

For George Pál and his Puppetoons in the 1950s, replacements were a trademark design trick, and many of his puppets have very fluid faces, full of stretch and squash. This needed dozens of replacements, all specifically and painstakingly plotted for the particular sequence.

Many of George Pál's short films feature dozens of perfectly synchronised soldiers, the accuracy of which might have defeated more traditional stop-motion puppets. Have a look at his spectacular *Rhythm in the Ranks* (1941).

Stylised movement > Replacements > Eyes

With puppets you can take away the nose in the design, and they still work. Remove the mouth as well and there's still life, but remove the eyes, and there's nothing. A single look from expressive eyes can make words redundant. Therefore, if you design a puppet with fixed eyes or no more than black dots then you are limiting that character's potential performance. Two black pinpricks can be just enough to give a puppet some life, giving the face a focus, and an outlet for expression, but the more detail in the eyes the better. The expression 'the eyes are the window to the soul' is very hackneyed but it is true. If black dots are right for the design then you will need to give that character particularly expressive body language. This works well for a character such as Bob the Builder who is extremely physical. His spirited body language compensates for a satisfyingly simple face.

Levels of subtlety

The type of eyes you use can have an enormous impact on the way in which a character will perform and move. It should therefore be one of the first decisions you make about a puppet. Fixed, generic eyes are honest and straightforward and allow little subterfuge, which may be appropriate for the story. If you want subtlety, black dots are unlikely to work. If you give the puppet realistic representations of human eyes, with enough whites to allow movement of the pupils, then you give the character a huge range of expression. Alternatively, a face held rigid but with the eyes slowly moving to one side immediately gives some subtext and depth.

Any movement in the eyes suggests a thought process, and with moving eyes you can start to play with focus, and just as importantly, lack of focus. Add slowly blinking lids and the amount of expression is magnified enormously. Add eyebrows, and you have an unlimited range of expression.

▶

Bob the Builder 1999–present

Studio
HIT Entertainment

Bob the Builder may have a simple face but replacement eye blinks, an opening mouth, and lively body language give him an abundance of character.

If you go to the trouble and expense of creating such a detailed puppet, make sure that you use it to its full potential. This means planning your storyboard and method of shooting to allow for shots that reveal the eye acting. Ensure that you stress where a movement begins and then show its full progression. Usually a movement will begin with the eyes focusing on something, showing the intent of a move to come. Then this translates into the body. All this is time-consuming, and therefore expensive, so keep asking yourself how subtle you need your characters' performances to be.

Some schedules and budgets may not allow for complex eyes, as struggling to keep eyes in focus and stopping puppets from making wayward glances all takes up valuable shooting time. There is, however, a magical moment as you place a puppet on the set and focus the eyes. Suddenly, with the eyes in focus looking somewhere with deliberation, a lump of clay or brass armature and cloth becomes a character. It is an exciting transformation.

Life's a Zoo 2008–present

Studio
Cuppa Coffee

The characters from *Life's a Zoo*, with their eyes suggesting some clear intent and focus, but look how the glasses rob the penguin character of that intent.

The Magic Projector 2007

animator
Chris Walsh

Two very simply sculpted characters from *The Magic Projector*, but their eyes still give them enormous expression.

Replacements > **Eyes** > Hands

Eye options

There are numerous ways to build eyes. Some puppets work with simple replacements, where the eye is literally poked out with a pin (not for the squeamish!) and replaced with a half shut or closed eye. Other puppets have glass or bead eyes set back in sockets and held in place by magnets, either with a range of eyelids added or, luxuriously, mechanical lids that can close quickly or slowly. You can even replace eyes to allow for bigger or smaller irises, which has an enormous effect on how the character is perceived in terms of friendliness or hostility. Some puppets have simple stick-on eyes, or even a magnetic rubber pupil; on some the eyes are drawn on – the range is endless. A trick much favoured by stop-motion animators is to wet the eyes with glycerine. This brings them to life amazingly, giving unexpected highlights. Eyes are a fiddly, time-consuming part of the animation process, but worth getting right.

Alternatively, and depending on the character, you could hide the eyes behind sunglasses or a mask, which, while speeding up the animation, also brings a distinct feeling of coldness. This can actually be very effective for characters with a darker nature, as nothing is given away and this can make the viewer feel vulnerable and exposed. A prime example of this is the unsettling effect achieved by replacing eyes with buttons on many of the characters in *Coraline* (2009).

Madame Tutli-Putli, a staggering film from 2007, has human eyes seamlessly matted onto a stop-motion puppet, and the effect is uncanny, disturbing and very, very beautiful. It would have been too disturbing, though, if the face had been more realistic, but Madame Tutli-Putli is still clearly a puppet, with roughly sculpted face and hands, and a glorious fixed smudge of a mouth. The moist human eyes perfectly express the sense of dread and fear of her situation. There is no need for words. This technique was inevitably time consuming but it is a remarkable and moving film.

▶

Gargoyle 2006

animator
Michael Cusack

A still from Michael Cusack's eerie film *Gargoyle*, showing the title character deprived of literal eyes and thus 'looking' with his whole body.

▲

Madame Tutli-Putli 2007

directors
Chris Lavis and
Maciek Szczerbowksi

Here we see Madame Tutli-Putli
and her amazing human eyes,
matted onto a beautifully
simple puppet.

Replacements > **Eyes** > Hands

Hands are a major form of expression and need special consideration when developing a puppet. Traditionally, whether for reasons of economics or ease of drawing, cartoon characters often find themselves with three fingers and a thumb. This little cheat is fine for 2D animation, but stop-motion puppets' fingers do have a practical **prehensile** purpose as well as an aesthetic one and it is therefore desirable to have five digits if possible. This is because it is not only much easier to hold props with four fingers and the all-important thumb, but the range of expression is considerably wider than with three fingers and a thumb.

Handy hints

The complex mechanics for expressive hands are expensive so do consider just how important and significant the hands are for your characters and the film. It is well worth going through your script to decide just what will be required of your characters' hands and design them accordingly. Here are some key points to consider:

▶ Wire fingers can work well for very simple puppets, but they have a limited life and can seldom be straightened once bent.

▶ Silicon has excellent durability but allows nothing to stick to it. Animators, therefore, often have to resort to pins, invisible thread and even superglue – all of which slow filming down. Silicon can also develop tears when fingers are left in extreme positions for a long period.

▶ Clay, by its nature, can produce good chunky comedy hands, but this makes it difficult to sustain long elegant fingers. They simply fall to pieces.

Prehensile (chiefly of an animal's limb or tail): capable of grasping.

- During the filming process hands will suffer wear and tear and fingers will break. This means that you will need several pairs.

- Due to their small size hands will always be fiddly to animate, and animators dread the sound of a falling prop as it slips through a puppet's fingers. Placing small magnets embedded in the palms can help.

- Stop-motion characters are often based on animals, with paws that limit expression and grip. If you have animal characters think carefully about what their paws will need to do.

- Some characters with stylised hands still manage to be expressive through rhythm and pacing rather than actual articulation. The *Rick and Steve* films are a great example of this as the characters are based on simple children's toys with fixed curved hands, which have become an essential feature of the animation.

As with so many aspects of stop-motion, it's about the balance between the aesthetic and the practical. All this will test how much you enjoy working with small things; but then a gesture, beautifully expressed through an eloquent hand movement, is hugely satisfying.

◄

In the Fall of Gravity 2008

animator
Ron Cole

Here we see three puppets with beautifully expressive hands from the film *In the Fall of Gravity*. As with people, puppets often convey meaning through body language, especially their hands. They can express enormous inner feeling when they are used thoughtfully but insensitive, fussy treatment can distract from the performance.

Puppet size

There is no standard size for a stop-motion puppet. This is because the appropriate size is governed by the practicalities of the individual film, the studio – and the animator's hand. If the puppet is to have complicated mechanics in the head, it may help the **fabricators** if the puppets are larger than normal. If this is the case, then bear in mind that everything escalates once you decide to have larger puppets. For example, it will require larger sets, and therefore a larger space in the studio. The size of the puppet will also dictate the required strength of the joints – and very strong joints can be more difficult to animate.

Similarly, very small puppets are fiddly and awkward. It is often difficult to include the required detail in the sculpting and sufficiently fine texture in the costumes. Very small puppets can also sometimes necessitate animating with toothpicks when the animator's fingers simply aren't nimble enough.

Being practical

A practical size is usually dictated by simple ergonomics. Ask yourself whether you can you hold the puppet comfortably and steadily in one hand, and control it easily with the other. Most puppets end up somewhere around 22–30cm (9–12 inches). This scale should allow sufficiently detailed close-ups as well as controllable armatures. Some animators just can't manage to manipulate a small mouth, for example, without knocking the puppet, due to their own chunky fingers. Do think very carefully about the size implications of your puppets and how that will affect the sets and the studio space. It's all related.

▶

Tales from the Powder Room
2002

animator
Darren Burgess

Darren Burgess animating a character from his *Tales from the Powder Room* – these puppets are certainly a practical size.

Fabricators are a team of artists who look after all aspects of creating puppets, from the detailed armatures to the tailored costumes and subtle painting of the skins.

▲

Next 1989

animator
Barry Purves

Here I am animating William Shakespeare – indicating a comfortable size of puppet.

Tip: Very large puppets

If a puppet gets too big, necessitating other animators or external manipulation, some animators worry about the lack of control. Much of the beauty of stop-motion is in its direct intimacy, with the puppets cradled in one hand. However, sometimes very big puppets are necessary to a story. For example, the large were-rabbit puppet in *Wallace and Gromit: The Curse of the Were-Rabbit* needed more than one animator, and its features were controlled externally by discreet cables. This had the added benefit of leaving the fur untouched.

Hands > **Puppet size** > Clay

Clay and Plasticine are ideal materials to begin animating with as they are considerably cheaper than armatured puppets. To animate with clay, however, you do need one skill that other animators do not: simply, you have to be able to sculpt. You also need an ability to keep a mental and physical image of the master shape in your head, and in your hands, as you resculpt the figure each frame.

Clay is flexible and solid enough to act as its own armature with small moves, but more radical moves require resculpting and this fact has defeated many animators. The effort needed for sculpting can take away an animator's feeling for the movement. Due to the material, the characters have an inevitable chunkiness which is definitely part of their charm. You'll also find that most clay characters develop good substantial feet, as that is the only way to make them stand up. If you are planning elegant or delicate characters for your film, clay may not be appropriate.

Fine textures such as fur or wrinkles should also be avoided in this medium, as the continuity will be impossible to maintain from frame to frame. Scale, with clay, also becomes an issue as the weight of the material can very quickly become cumbersome with large puppets. Despite all these limitations, however, clay characters are also amazingly versatile and joyously hands-on; you can both feel and see the results of your animation.

Beaver Creek 2008

animator
Ian Timothy

Twigs the Beaver from 14-year-old Ian Timothy's impressive *Beaver Creek* films.

▲

Faust 1994

animator
Jan Švankmajer

Clay used for a more disturbing
effect. A character from Jan
Švankmajer's dazzling *Faust*;
a film full of many different bold
techniques.

Jan Švankmajer

Jan Švankmajer produces extraordinarily
visceral films. Not only does he push the
possibilities of clay, getting all manner of
meaning out of his transformations, but he
also boldly mixes clay with objects, offal,
and literally anything. His breathtakingly
daring films are testament again, that the
smallest object or the most unusual
material can be used to illustrate an
idea if that idea is good.

Physicality

Armatures are sometimes used for clay and animation puppets. This involves the clay being built up around the armature to form a flexible skin, sometimes even with preformed replacement mouths. This makes for a lighter puppet than using solid clay, and cuts out the need for repeated sculpting. However, it also means losing some of the stretch and squash capabilities of pure clay. For this reason, most puppets are solid clay, leading to a certain anatomical fluidity in the positioning of the joints. This is all part of the joy of working with clay and gives the characters a unique feel. Movement with such puppets can be subtle, but this can be very time-consuming. Clay is also fantastic for bold and brash statements. It is a very physical form of animation, and the technique is an essential part of it.

It is important to accept that fingerprints and variation of skin texture are an inseparable part of working with clay. This is something that should be enjoyed rather than hidden. Clay is also perfect if exaggeration is part of your puppet's performance. It may not be perfect for scenes of contained introspection, but if you want stretch and squash in your character, and anything to do with transformation, or morphing, clay is exactly the right material.

Clay animation is accessible and there is never any doubt that its characters have existed as part of the real world. With CG getting more and more astounding each day, it's satisfying that a mere lump of clay can still provide just as much fun to both animator and audience.

Recommended viewing

Have a look at the Gnome King sequences in *Return to Oz* (1985) for some imaginative use of clay animation. Here the technique of clay is totally appropriate for the character of a living mountain, constantly transforming. This was produced by Will Vinton Productions – Will's earlier short film, *The Great Cognito* (1982), features a string of remarkable and very detailed transformations, and showed clay's potential. Aardman Animation continues to push clay animation into all areas of imaginative sophistication, from the joyous *Morph* short films to full-length *Wallace and Gromit* feature films. Artists such as Joan Gratz in Canada use clay for painting, relishing the transformations and textures that clay offers. Have a look at her beautiful film, *Mona Lisa Descending a Staircase* (1992).

The puppets

▲

Morph 1977–2000

creators
Peter Lord and
David Sproxton

The versatile, ingenious, utterly simple, and constantly morphing Morph. The real props around him give an indication of his size.

Puppet size > **Clay** > Other techniques

If you find puppets either too literal or too expensive, but you still want to enjoy the tactile nature of stop-motion, there are several options open to you. Two of the main materials are sand and cut-outs, but don't think there is a limit to what can be animated. The techniques and tricks of stop-motion, of manipulating objects by hand, still apply whether the objects are tiny grains of sand, Post-it notes, or large chunks of scrap. The important idea is that you are using your hands to directly control the material. Anything that can be moved in a real space is capable of being part of an animated film, and producing exciting images.

Sand

The work of Vera Neubauer, Caroline Leaf and Joanna Priestley are all good examples of limited resources being used with a great deal of creativity. They certainly prove that it is not essential to have fully armatured puppets to produce powerful animation. All three use sand and various found objects to produce some beautifully textured films with a wonderful graphic quality. Caroline Leaf, in films such as *The Owl Who Married a Goose* (1974) and *The Metamorphosis of Mr Samsa* (1977), uses sand in combination with a light box, and the results are subtle and quite unique, mixing the graphic qualities of drawing with more dimensional work. Vera Neubauer's work, in films such as *Wheel of Life* (1996), has a more direct rawness and vitality, using sand that is still part of the beach, along with flotsam and jetsam. Both uses of sand are evocative and startling, and for all the visible technique still manage to communicate something profound and moving. Joanna Priestley's films use objects to produce very poignant and resonant collages. The shooting of these films must have been very satisfying, if a little unpredictable.

The Owl Who Married a Goose 1974

animator
Caroline Leaf

Here we see Caroline Leaf working on her sand film *The Owl Who Married a Goose*. The use of a light box turns the imagery into something very graphic and beautiful, almost a drawing, but with tangible texture.

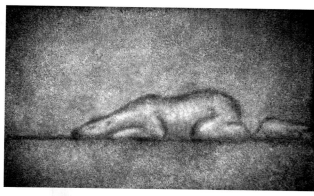

Bear with Me 2008

animator
Uriah Naeh

Rather than sand this film uses sea salt on glass, lit from underneath; it was created by Uriah Naeh at the Bezalel Academy of Arts and design in Jerusalem. The results are sublime and delicate.

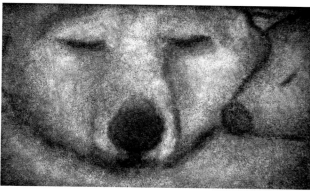

Cut-outs

Cut-outs are another unique form of animation, and the works of Lotte Reiniger, Michel Ocelot and Yuri Norstein show how extraordinarily rich and delicate this technique can be. It's still a very tactile technique, and once you have created the puppets you don't have to keep resculpting them, though a single character may have various elements that are changeable according to its movements.

To work with cut-outs you will need an acute eye for how a character best works as a silhouette, and how movement works in profile. Cut-outs mixed with a multiplane camera set-up literally add another dimension, and though computers are able to replicate such an effect easily, there are still effective examples today. A spin-off from *Bob the Builder,* called *Bob on Site* (2007) used a multiplane and cut-out insert, and the effect was rather beautiful, having real texture and depth.

It's a great joy to animate with cut-outs because you have all the pleasure of touching and manipulating puppets, but you don't have to worry about gravity or puppet joints. Of course there are other challenges, for example if you don't have the right paper, the characters can curl up. Fingerprints on the glass can slow production too. You also need extremely steady hands to move the paper pieces with precision. Animators often push the characters around with toothpicks as sometimes fingers are just too clumsy and maybe too sweaty, meaning that the pieces move as the hand is taken away. However, this is a very economical, personal and intimate form of animation, which is still a hands-on experience, and the results can give beautiful movement and gorgeous images.

When writing your script, constantly ask yourself whether your favoured technique can realise your ideas. If it can't, it's probably easier to revise the technique than the ideas, though often in animation they are so tightly knitted it is hard to separate them. However, it would be wrong to force an inappropriate technique on an idea.

▶

The author at work

A not very flattering still of myself working on a multiplane set-up, and surprisingly enjoyable it was too, although cramped and awkward.

▲

The Tale of Sir Richard 2006

animator
Peter Dodd

Peter Dodd's *The Tale of Sir Richard* used cut-outs with relief and filmed on different layers of glass. This film beautifully combines heavily textured, sculpted replacement pieces on different layers of glass. The effective results have a feel of puppets but without the expense of complicated armatures or the problems of gravity, and enormous budgets. It also retains the joy of the tactile process.

▶

Les Trois Inventeurs 1980

animator
Michel Ocelot

This exquisite still shows the delicate but very textural paper cut-outs.

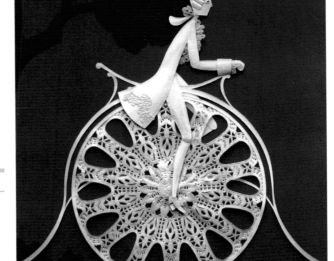

Clay > **Other techniques**

In Chapter 4 we'll look at all the preparation that is necessary for an easy shoot, and what sort of problems and pleasures you'll encounter on a film set. The process at this stage of film-making is very different from any other form of animation, with much more physicality involved. Detailed preparation before shooting will save so many problems later and is an essential stage to go through.

◄

Mary and Max 2009

animator
Adam Elliot

This still sums up everything that is glorious about stop-motion; enjoying all the elements of design, texture, lighting, colour, depth, detail and character to produce something very stylised but instantly credible and recognisable. Every element is working in harmony with the others.

Once a stop-motion film goes into production there are suddenly many other people involved, all overseen by the producer. The producer makes sure that the right people are doing the right things on time and within the budget. The producer also acts as a facilitator, allowing the director to realise their vision of the film whenever it is logistically possible. If the producer and director don't work together closely then the production can quickly become very fragmented.

Similarly, one of the director's key roles is to keep all of the different departments working towards the same end. The director must ensure that every decision is in keeping with the spirit and style of the film, and that every element is used to its fullest potential; that the **semiotics** of the film all work as one. A film needs a unified vision and thorough preparation is essential in achieving this.

Planning the logistics

Once the initial narrative and thematic ideas have been established, the next stage is the development of a script. Once the script has been completed the design process will continue and lead to the creation of a full storyboard. If there is sufficient budget this will be further developed into full **pre-visualisations** and the story reel.

Friendly Fire 2008

animator
Andy Kaiser

An early mood sketch from *Friendly Fire*, which suggests a look for the finished film, and helps everyone involved know what the director is hoping to achieve.

Semiotics is the study of signs and symbols and their use or interpretation.

Pre-visualisations (previz) are generally roughly animated digital recreations of the eventual film. There are basic sets and characters and the director is able to move the camera through this virtual world looking for perfect camera angles, which all help to inspire staging ideas ahead of being on the real set.

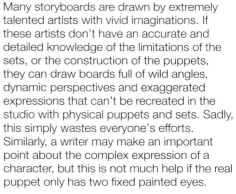

The purpose of all this is to ensure that everyone involved has a clear, shared understanding of the key elements required for the finished film. Through these various processes the director can anticipate what will work and what should be cut. This preparation is vital to avoid making costly impromptu decisions on the set. Stop-motion is so time-consuming that we really can't afford to shoot any more than is needed for the finished film. This requires very thorough and thoughtful preparation of every element of the film.

Many storyboards are drawn by extremely talented artists with vivid imaginations. If these artists don't have an accurate and detailed knowledge of the limitations of the sets, or the construction of the puppets, they can draw boards full of wild angles, dynamic perspectives and exaggerated expressions that can't be recreated in the studio with physical puppets and sets. Sadly, this simply wastes everyone's efforts. Similarly, a writer may make an important point about the complex expression of a character, but this is not much help if the real puppet only has two fixed painted eyes.

You will save yourself a great deal of time and trouble by working out the logistics of each scene during the writing and preparation process rather than trying to figure it out when you are on set.

Storyboards and pre-visualisation

A storyboard full of energy and detail will impress clients and tutors, and give an impression of what the feel of the film will be. However, the main purpose of the board is to provide a practical and accurate idea of how the finished film will turn out, and how each shot will fit into the overall picture. It is not necessarily about vivid artistic interpretations of a scene, but it is about the angle the director would prefer to shoot a scene from, which is important for the camera operator and set dressers to know in advance. The storyboard is a vital common point of reference for everyone involved with the film. Of course, if you're performing all these roles yourself you will still need the same very clear pre-production planning.

Storyboards, by their very nature, are static, and may therefore need several drawings to convey the important action of a scene. You'll find it easier if you work with one shot per page of the board, as it becomes easier to see what effect the removal or addition of a shot will have, and how shots then sit next to each other. In this way your board will be practical and adaptable.

Creating very rough CG characters in a representation of the geography of a scene in a digital previz allows the director to move a virtual camera around. The previz provide many options, and help the director get an approximate feel of the film before committing to any major and costly decisions. The use of movement in previz also lets you gauge whether the rhythm, the timing and the grammar of the film are working.

Usually, when the director is happy with the previz or the storyboard, they are edited as a complete story reel, using approximate timings. This is where it becomes apparent what is working well and what needs changing. Spending time in careful preparation at the beginning of the film-making process will mean that more expensive studio time is well spent later on.

Mutt 2008

director
Glen Hunwick

Here we see several loose sketches from Glen Hunwick's *Mutt*. These initial sketches are invaluable in working out angles and compositions as they can be directly translated to the finished film (left).

Tip: Thinking ahead

When you are writing the story, drawing the storyboard, or working on the digital previz, it's all too easy to forget the realities of stop-motion. For example, a script can easily describe a scene of wild, energetic choreography but bringing that to life is very much more difficult. While you should never rein in your imagination when writing, it is important to constantly be aware that you are dealing with very physical characters, and the script and storyboard must reflect this.

Working with others > Sets

Building sets is a hugely appealing aspect of stop-motion and gives people great satisfaction, harking back to playing with dolls' houses, train sets and model building as a child. There always has been, and always will be, something inherently satisfying about standing in front of a solid miniature world. If you have an eye for detail and texture, stop-motion is definitely for you.

Practical requirements

Any set has to accommodate lots of important requirements. For example, they must allow access for the animator as well as the cameras and lights. They must also be sufficiently stable to withstand animators stretching in and leaning on the surfaces during every frame; not allowing anything to wobble or sag or bend during the shot. Even more challengingly, a set designer must make what is essentially a flat table top look like a convincing interior or epic vista.

Chiodo Brothers set

Here we see a set at a comfortable working height, full of the clutter that is an essential part of stop-motion. It's also interesting to note cameraman Rex Reed lighting a similar set alongside the animator getting prepared – a small set can quickly become crowded.

All manner of theatrical tricks such as gauzes, false perspectives, and clever painting go some way to achieving a grand scale, but it has to be said that CG can create the most amazing and spectacular landscapes, certainly beyond anything that can be built practically in a normal studio and with restricted budgets. If your film is all about sweeping landscapes or complex cityscapes, do think about CG. Alternatively, you may want to film your puppet characters against a green screen and composite them into a CG environment. This is certainly a practical solution but it is often not as much fun as creating real sets and working with techniques such as false perspective to make them look bigger.

If you do choose to rely on false perspectives to help create a sense of scale then you must think carefully about all the angles that you will use. The illusion can be easily destroyed and maintaining it requires careful planning in the storyboards. To make it easier to maintain the illusion of scale, stop-motion sets are usually built with a 'front' – this not only helps spell out the geography very clearly, but it helps practically with all the rigging and the lighting. If you have a set that will be shot from 360 degrees, all the walls will need to be removed and probably the lighting changed for each set-up. This will require more space and time on the studio floor.

Exercise: Aspect ratios

When designing the sets it's essential to consider the aspect ratio the film will be shot in, and to try to map out every composition in advance. Films for television used to be traditionally screened in a 4:3 ratio, but now the shape is usually 16:9, which more closely resembles the human visual field. In the cinema the shape can be even more extreme. Widescreen is certainly dynamic. Try staging a simple two-way conversation in different ratios and see how that affects the storytelling and the number of shots needed.

Credibility

If a set is too clean and flat then it can easily disrupt the illusion of scale. Texture, stop-motion's great friend, can help mitigate this effect. Introducing some essential weathering to the sets can also help. Sets need to look lived in and you'll be surprised what a difference a bit of shading in corners or the odd scratch can make. The same applies to costumes. As always, it's the little unexpected touches and imperfections that make a set and a character credible to the viewer.

For this reason, animators usually prefer working on real sets, where we can respond to the environment and introduce tiny but telling details. Working in a green screen vacuum is exactly that – a vacuum. It's harder to feel part of the scene, and to some extent the animation becomes like a layer of a cel animation or an element in a CG film. Time and time again we come back to enjoying stop-motion because it is all there right in front of us and we can touch it. Being part of this small world it is not hard to imagine how the characters respond and behave.

A whole new world

As every single item has to be created from scratch, why not enjoy giving the sets character and style? Sets, like all the other elements of your film, should contribute to and reflect the overarching story, characters and themes. When you are designing, try to create a whole new credible world for the story, where everything works seamlessly together. For example, remember that stop-motion sets often don't need to match the proportions of real human architecture. This is simply because the characters are often animals or other fantasy creations with a wide range of anatomical proportions. If a door is designed for human proportions, the chances are it won't fit all the characters in your film.

Much of the success of the Wallace and Gromit films depends on the details in the sets, which are often only apparent in repeated viewings. Consider how much the dog bones on Gromit's wallpaper say about him. Just as there is often a visual shorthand for puppets (such as haughty characters being portrayed by tall, spiky puppets) so the colour and shapes used in sets can be reflective of the stories they tell. Of course, however fanciful you get with the sets, it's essential that the characters stand out in front. The sets support the characters, not the other way round.

I always laugh when I hear that a form of animation is dying. They've been saying for years that stop-motion is dead. But a few of us are still around.

Mike Johnson

▲

Electreecity 2008

animators
Sarah Davison and
Sarah Duffield-Harding

A beautifully stylised, simple and imaginative set. This scene makes creative use of texture, and gives a familiar image of a tree a fresh perspective.

Tip: Doors

Remember that there will be elements on the set that will need to be animated at specific times, such as doors, but for the rest of the scene they need to be rock solid. Magnets can help with this or small hinges that can be tensioned. Nothing ruins a shot more than a character walking towards a door, and the door twitching before it is opened. This is usually caused by the animator's clumsiness. Everything has to be fixed solidly to the set, and yet still be free to move as necessary. Solving this requires ingenuity and to enjoy stop-motion it certainly helps to enjoy this kind of problem solving.

Working with others > **Sets** > Costume

Set points – things to think about

▶ **Life beyond the frame**

Although most sets are based on a table top, it doesn't take much imagination to suggest life continuing not just either side of the frame, but also above and below it. While designing for the camera, don't forget to allow room for your characters, especially characters with prominent shadows, to walk out of shot. This is particularly helpful when you are dealing with vehicles. Too often I've animated a car to the edge of the set, and half of it still remains in shot. Again, these issues should be considered carefully during pre-production planning.

▶ **Incidental movement**

Any details built into the set (such as leaves or papers on the floor, or swinging doors) that can react to characters as they pass by can be extremely helpful. They can aid the illusion of a tangible movement, and plant the characters credibly in their world. Adding effects in post-production such as mists or moving clouds or shadows also helps.

▶ **Angles**

Make sure that the tripod and geared head can go low enough to get all the angles needed to realise the planned storyboard.

Hide and Seek 2007

animators
Kerry Drumm and
Aaron Wood

Puppets from Kerry Drumm and Aaron Wood's student film *Hide and Seek*, showing the uncovered perforated steel set perfect for supporting puppets with magnets, and then disguised to look like floorboards.

Foregrounds

If your set contains a foreground element, such as a lawn with long grass or flowers, this will look great but may be a nightmare to work with. You will have to lean over the foreground for each frame, probably knocking the flowers or leaving prints in the grass. Spraying the grass with hairspray may help, as would making the flowers very rigid. However, if you are shooting on digital it might be easier to treat the foreground piece as a separate element. Shoot it with a piece of green screen behind ahead of the shot, and then remove it. It can then be replaced in post-production. This technique can solve many problems but does prevent the animator from seeing the complete picture and does limit the use of camera moves.

Set height

The most convenient height for a set is usually level with the animator's waist. This height will normally minimise any physical strain. While considering the height of the set do make sure that the camera equipment is suitably adaptable, and the camera can sit in a position appropriate for the viewpoint of the film. I worked on one low set where the unimaginative cameraman shot everything from his eye level, rather than at the eye level of the characters in the set. It was as if God was looking down, surveying the whole scene, giving a feel not intended in the script.

Costume

A puppet in a gloriously well-fitting and detailed costume can be very expressive and add so much to both the character and the film as a whole. However, before you start making wonderfully elaborate costumes for your puppets, there are some points that need to be considered.

As with every other aspect of the puppet, the costumes will be touched in every frame, and they need to be designed accordingly to prevent constant twitching. One solution is to have double-sided tape to stick the costume to the puppet. However, clothes must be able to move freely with the puppet, not restricting the joints. Costumes must also allow access to the armature so that the animator can adjust their tension when necessary. The seams that allow this access should be as invisible as possible.

Another effect of touching the costume every frame is that they inevitably become dirty, or certain fabrics will 'bobble'. So think carefully before you give your main character a pristine white, woolly outfit!

▲

Gargoyle 2006

animator
Michael Cusack

Much care has been taken to make this dress hang with weight and substance.

Fabric

Nothing betrays the scale of a puppet more than fabric. The printed fabric that looks delicate when used for a full-size human outfit will often look like thick, rough hessian when used on a miniature puppet and seen in close-up on screen. It is therefore very important to carefully select a fabric that will work at the scale of your film. For example, if your fabric is too lightweight, then it is unlikely to have enough weight to hang properly. Clever tailoring and wiring can help here. It's likely that any fabric you buy will have to be dyed, or printed, or given some help to make it look appropriate. As with the sets, weathering and distressing the costumes will help them look lived in. On a large shoot, you'll probably have duplicates of the main characters, so be careful to make a design that can be duplicated. Details such as feathers and fur will need a lot of care to ensure that they are in scale with the rest of the film.

Tomorrow 2009

animator
Bob Lee

This still from Bob Lee's film *Tomorrow* shows the detail and distressing of the costume. Not only does it look credible, it gives the character an immediate history.

Life and movement

Costumes have to suit the characters, and they have to look appropriate in terms of scale and texture. Just as importantly, they should also be used to help the movement of the character. Everything in animation is about giving the suggestion of life and movement, and costumes are no different. When a stop-motion character is supposed to be running their clothes will not naturally trail behind them and so the animators must create this effect. Even something as simple as an animatable scarf flapping behind a running character will help give an illusion of momentum, although it is extra work to animate.

As you develop each scene, think about how costume might promote or undermine the illusion you are creating. For example, if the scene involves dozens of ballroom dancers packed tightly together, just reaching the puppets will be hard enough. Also, dresses are notoriously difficult to work with as they have to be lifted for access to the legs, and then repositioned, hopefully in the same place. For a ball scene you might have to create a very different method of animating the puppet, perhaps using solid dresses. Always try to think how the costume will both hinder and help the movement.

Madame Tutli-Putli 2007

directors
Chris Lavis and
Maciek Szczerbowski

The very convincing and detailed costume and accessories worn by Madame Tutli-Putli don't betray their scale at all. They also match the detailed and nicely weathered set, which must have had some very ingenious access points for the animators.

Practicalities

Shoes are an essential part of any costume, unless the whole film is in close-up, but they are also something of a problem. Every puppet has to be attached to the set in some way and whatever method you choose will affect the design of the shoes (see page 85). If you are using magnets, you'll need to incorporate a flat metal base, which will be awkward if you are thinking of high heels. If you are using tie-downs, consider how the screw will work with the shoe. As always, it's important to accommodate the various technical issues of stop-motion into your designs. Overcoming these challenges can be a joy in itself.

Costumes are part of the design process and can contribute enormously to the palette and look of a film, with even the smallest detail helping the fantasy and anthropomorphic ideas. If you are working with totally clay characters, you are unlikely to be able to maintain much detail, shape or finesse in a clay costume, as this will have to be resculpted or touched up more times than it is worth. Costumes are not just something that cover the puppets – they can help the narrative and characters, but always think of the practical issues involved.

▶

Friendly Fire 2009

animator
Andy Kaiser

Here we see designer Joergen Knoll with the costumes needed for the puppets in *Friendly Fire*. Not only did they have to be convincing miniatures, they had to match the full-scale costumes of the live-action actors.

Colour

As we've already seen, when a set is prepared and the camera is in place it is usually far too late to make changes to the puppets, costumes, props or sets. Therefore, another vital element of your film that must be decided during pre-production is the colour scheme. This is where CG has a distinct advantage as a quick tweak of a few buttons can change the virtual set from red to green. To a considerable extent, especially with digital films, the tones, hues and colours of a whole scene can be altered in post-production. But this is not the case in stop-motion and so all these decisions have to be made during pre-production.

Many animators prefer this way of working, as it means that they must think through and cement their vision of the film early on. Once the sets, puppets and costumes have been made there is no room for a change of heart. This should lead to a cohesive design, even for films that take years to produce, as all the key decisions are made early on and there is very little room to deviate from them. All the designed elements of your film will work together to strengthen the integrity of the whole, leaving the main spontaneity to come from the performances.

Colour palettes

Colour can contribute much more than just pleasing aesthetics – particular colours can produce various different emotional responses in the audience. This is especially important in children's films, where bright colours are usually the order of the day. Like texture, which we can enjoy so much in stop-motion, colour detail comes very easily in this medium. Puppets can be painted with an endless range of colour and gradations and textures. However, as with costumes, the puppet will be touched every frame and pale colours will show any marks easily. Therefore, unless you have the schedule to constantly clean the puppets, do think carefully before choosing a very light palette. You will also need to work very closely with the designers to make sure that the colours of the puppets stand out against the backgrounds. Any puppet and set will be subject to maintenance during a long shoot, so be aware that complex colour schemes take considerable effort to match.

▶

L'Oiseau 2009

animator
Samuel Yal

Four stills from Samuel Yal's
L'Oiseau using wonderfully bold
colour schemes and strikingly
uncluttered compositions.
© Double Mètre Animation

Lavatory Lovestory 2007

writer/director
Konstantin Bronzit

Konstantin Bronzit's Oscar-
nominated *Lavatory Lovestory*
contains a very effective
narrative use of colour. When
a lavatory attendant finds a
beautiful bouquet of flowers left
in her tip jar it brightens up her
otherwise quiet, monochrome
existence – prompting her to
track down her shy suitor.

In Chapter 5 we will look at how all of the technical elements involved with stop-motion affect the storytelling and the film itself and how they are just as important as the animation.

Since we have to create absolutely everything from scratch, it's important to make the most of every single element, letting them contribute to the film, rather than just being an afterthought, mere decoration, or simply architecture. Try to give every cut, every framing, every piece of music some resonance to the overall narrative and theme. Animation is not solely about moving characters; it is about storytelling, and every element can help that story to be told.

◀

Wallace and Gromit:
The Curse of the Were-Rabbit
2005

animator
Aardman

Stop-motion audiences appreciate that every tiny detail of the films is painstakingly created. In this case, a rabbit's eyeline changes courtesy of a carefully wielded toothpick.

Preparations > **Tools and techniques** > Movement and performance

Once you have moved a real object in real space, the preceding pose has gone forever. Although it is captured flat as a still image, the real three-dimensional move has gone for good. With drawn and computer animation the previous moves still exist very clearly and the subsequent move can be adjusted and fine-tuned accordingly. Your reaction to this element of imprecision is probably quite a good reflection of how well you are suited to stop-motion. A lot of animators feel much happier and safer when their animation is backed up by mathematics, with the chance of several, progressively more subtle takes and with the opportunity to actually work out a move before doing it. For some, however, mathematics gets in the way of performance, and the hand memory, (and muscle memory), and most important of all, instinct, are all that is needed for good animation. For many stop-motion animators our love of the medium is about that abstract quality – performance – and no amount of precise measurements and refining can make good animation if there is no natural instinct for performance, storytelling and acting. If you feel daunted by the idea of instinctive performance, then stop-motion, without its technical safety net, may not be right for you. But if you find this hint of the unknown exciting then you might just have found the right medium to tell your story.

The appeal of this raw way of working may mean that you begin to feel a little frustrated when technology comes between you and your character's performance. However, the technology of sophisticated playback systems certainly does make life much easier. Animators are sometimes nervous about tinkering too much with puppets in between the frames, and usually take a big breath before removing a puppet from the set in order to make some maintenance necessary to save a shot. They are worried about breaking some through line of action and never getting the puppet back into position. For most of stop-motion's history, getting the puppet back in the exact position was a question of a highly developed muscle memory, a few surface gauges or similar devices, and outrageous fortune. Playbacks of the preceding frame, especially with 'onion skins' that allow you to see the previous frame layered with the existing shot, have made this very much easier.

Les Triplettes de Belleville
2003

writer/director
Sylvain Chomet

A quickly rotating wheel might appear to be standing still or moving backwards due to one spoke of the wheel moving forward into its predecessor's position exactly, or just behind it. The viewer's eye then wrongly makes the assumption that the spoke has moved backwards. Drawn and CG animators can blur the image with speed lines to help avoid this. It's not quite so easy with stop-motion.

Strobing

Strobing is an unhelpful illusion whereby an object or character judders distractingly, or appears to move backwards, even though it has been physically moved forwards. This occurs when the overall direction of the movement has been interrupted. It is an especially common problem during camera moves when the speed of the move is not consistent, incrementally, with the character's movement within the frame, causing it to shift about within the frame. For example, a quickly rotating wheel might appear to be standing still or moving backwards due to one spoke of the wheel moving forwards into its predecessor's position exactly, or just behind it. The viewer's eye then wrongly makes the assumption that the spoke has moved backwards.

We have to take special care to avoid this in stop-motion as we cannot usually blur the image, which is always helpful in suggesting a direction of movement. Various tricks can help, such as adding trailing items suggesting the direction of movement, or giving each spoke a distinguishing detail – but it is essential not only to be aware of how a character has moved through its spatial environment, but also how it has moved through the camera framing. Make the direction clear and consistent.

Similarly, walking characters are particularly susceptible to jerkiness. It's easy to spend so much effort on getting the feet and leg positions right that you physically knock the torso back in the odd frames without realising it, whereas the torso should be constantly moving forwards. Any conflicting movement will judder horribly.

Single or double frames

One important decision you must make is whether to shoot in single or double frames (ones or twos). In other words, should you have 24–25 different individual frames per second or should you make a movement only every two or three frames? More often than not, the choice to shoot on double frames is a choice made out of economy rather than artistry. It is possible to 'get away' with shooting on doubles, but it is often exactly that: 'getting away with it'.

Watching a piece of doubles animation is usually harder work and very much less enjoyable than a piece of singles, as the viewer's brain has to fill in missing information. Of course financial needs and schedules sometimes necessitate shooting on doubles, and with a first film you may not have a choice, but be aware that it can restrict the quality of animation. With just 12 frames per second you are unlikely to

be able to do much softening at the ends of moves, or subtle quivers of a lip, for example, or a delicate tremble of the hand. On the other hand a staccato effect may be appropriate to your film or characters. Doubles also give a certain raw energy that might be right for the scene, but if you are trying to get a lyrical quality, the more frames the better. With 25 frames per second you can put in so much more detail and information, leading to more sophisticated and rounded animation that flows as credibly as possible. Of course, there are some actions for which even 25 frames per second aren't enough; such as a woodpecker in action. Drawn and CG animators would definitely smudge the animation here. With stop-motion, we'd probably move the head back and forth through a greater extreme in single frames, and help show the effect of the pecking through wobbling tree trunks and leaves.

Exercise: Singles and doubles

A perfect way to demonstrate the difference between singles and doubles is to divide a given length into half centimetres. Move one object half a centimetre each frame. Move another object side by side but a centimetre every other frame. They will both be, in effect, travelling the same distance at the same speed, but the difference in quality of movement is amazing.

Tools and techniques

In this way, it is sometimes the technique you are using that dictates whether to shoot on singles or doubles. For example, sculpting a clay figure 25 times per second is not just labour intensive, it also doubles the amount of unwanted movement and 'boiling' on the surface. Similarly, your puppet may have a restricted armature that can't actually cope with the finesse of fine movements, and so bigger double frame movements have to be the answer. There is also nothing to stop you mixing singles and doubles in the same action. For example, you could start a heavy object moving with a series of tiny single frame increments, and then once the object is up and moving you can switch to double frames, but you will notice the difference. You'll notice the difference too, if you shoot a close-up in doubles although you can get away with it more easily in long shots. Many animators are reluctant to shoot anything in double frames because they want to make everything flow (though this is not the same as making everything balletic and lyrical). With a double frame you are immediately putting a break in this flow.

At the heart of this question is the size of the increments between frames in proportion to the size of the frame. If the increments cover a tiny amount of the frame, and link to the previous frame, you'll have smooth animation. If the increment covers a large amount of the frame, the animation will fall to pieces, as it stops relating to the previous frame. There is such a difference between close-up animating and wide-shot animating, and shooting in doubles doesn't help us one bit. The best approach is to analyse the sort of movement you want from your characters, and the capabilities of your puppets. If you have the option then it will help to learn to shoot in singles and then make your choice after that to suit your style.

Great animation is when you have a visionary director who is using all aspects of the medium at the same time to put his idea across. That's... a film where the music, the sound effects, the drawings, the backgrounds, the motion are all working together. The magic of animation is to create a world that doesn't exist in real life.... All of the artifice falls away and you're left with the sheer joy of life.

Stephen Worth

There is something very comforting about having a camera on a stop-motion set. We are the only animators that generally get to see one, and it reinforces the whole idea that stop-motion is a performance, and that there is an audience. Other animators must feel a sense of detachment as they work on their camera-less light boxes and computers. For the stop-motion animator, the camera is a continual presence, and we should be very respectful of it. It gives a focus to the proceedings, and the sound of a shutter being exposed is an essential part of the process.

Of course, the physicality of stop-motion means that the camera can be both a blessing and a curse as it can get in the way. For this reason, stop-motion animators develop an odd body language as they work twisted around the camera – leading to many aching backs. Many older films were shot on glorious 35mm cameras, but they are bulky and awkward, and the building of the sets had to take into consideration the presence of, and access needed by, the camera. The trend now is to shoot on small digital still cameras – this makes an animator's life much easier. The tiny camera can go right into the sets and into awkward angles that were never previously possible. This has an enormous impact on the way we tell our stories.

Many traditional animators miss the imperfections and the richness of real film, though few miss the bulky cameras on set. The size of a digital camera, and the instant feedback they can provide, are also very animator friendly. They offer extraordinary potential for manipulation of the images. Digital cameras certainly make the whole process more accessible to beginners and those with limited resources.

Physical limitations

In stop-motion we cannot avoid the fact that there must be a camera in front of the set, and any camera moves have to be animated frame by frame. This raises problems of access to the set, shadows caused by their movements, and the space taken up by tracking equipment. All of this is undeniably challenging. However, as is so often the case with stop-motion, developing inventive solutions to these problems is incredibly satisfying.

Camera moves have been slowly introduced during the history of stop-motion. At first, the shots were set up like a theatre stage, with the characters moving within the static frame. Later, a few handheld moves with imprecise increments appeared. This led to the camera being placed on tracks, which allowed it to travel sideways following a puppet, or even track into a set. The next stage was the introduction of complicated and cumbersome motion control rigs, which allowed the camera to move on several axes. These were initially manual, and often highly ingenious, but the introduction of computers to the process allowed the camera to repeat the movements with precision. It is now possible to achieve several passes accurately, increasing the potential for using special effects.

Cameras can now be relatively mobile, but the planning of camera moves is time consuming, and they must be meticulously plotted beforehand. This can make the animator feel that they must keep up with the camera rather than the camera following the movement of the characters. This cramps the animation, as the animator has to make sure that the character is at a given mark at a given frame to be in the shot and in focus; thus killing some spontaneity.

Friendly Fire 2009

director
Andy Kaiser

Here we see a snorkel lens allowing access to the miniature trenches set of *Friendly Fire*. A snorkel lens, much like an inverted periscope, can be added to the camera and allow the lens into situations where the camera body could not get.

Recommended viewing

Have a look at the astonishing effects in the short film *Friendly Fire*, which were all achieved in camera, on film, with absolutely no digital manipulation. The director, Andy Kaiser, wanted the film to reflect his love of silent classics such as *Nosferatu* (1922), where the image is vibrant and alive with inconsistencies of exposure. Film provided an erratic warmth that the precision of digital does not provide, unless it is deliberately put in. Once again, it is the mistakes and the lack of total precision that give stop-motion its heart, and a director must make the most of this.

Practicalities > The camera > Lighting

Movement and pacing

Most films are now shot with high-definition digital cameras, which allow some movement to be put into the shot during post-production. This can include zooming in slightly in order to accent a portion of the frame, or a shift to alter the composition of the shot and draw the audience's attention to something relevant. However, these shots should be treated with care as they can easily appear very obvious and flat, especially when these post-production movements are seen alongside physical camera moves. This is because the post-production moves create no shift in parallax, which is one of the real beauties of working in a physical space. Parallax is the effect whereby the position or direction of an object appears to differ when viewed from different positions.

The more use you can make of the depth of a real set, the more effective the camera moves will be. Imagine a puppet standing alone in a white space with no detail. A camera move would not be effective as there would be little to suggest any changing perspective. But in the same set, put in foreground pieces and long corridors trailing away and the slightest camera move will read effectively. Camera moves can also help the rhythm and pacing of a film tremendously, although they can be very difficult to achieve in stop-motion. The famous model train sequence in the Wallace and Gromit film *The Wrong Trousers* (1993) is a great example of pacing. This sequence has been helped by ingenious blurred backgrounds (both painted as blurred wallpaper and moved during the exposure), giving the impression of speed.

However, if your story is dependent on fast and complicated camera moves, stop-motion may not be the easiest way to go. Remember, a CG and drawn camera can go absolutely anywhere, but a stop-motion camera not only has to be animated each frame, its access is also limited by its physical presence. This can, of course, be overcome by clever set building and sympathetic budgets and schedules but it is an important element that directly affects the narrative.

In the theater, while you recognized that you were looking at a house, it was a house in quotation marks. On screen, the quotation marks tend to be blotted out by the camera.

Arthur Miller

Tools and techniques

▲

Amelia Jane 2006

art director
Lynne Pritchard

The simple, uncluttered but striking set of *Amelia Jane*, with a small digital camera making access easy.

Recommended viewing

The camerawork on *Madame Tutli-Putli* (see page 102) is extraordinary, with deliberately erratic movements plotted to echo hand-held live-action camerawork. It gives a very fluid, spontaneous feel to the story, as if the camera is responding to the puppets. Animation moves tend to be smooth, because of the way they are plotted, but the moves in this film are appropriately loose and dynamic.

When you are working on your own camera moves remember that they are the same as animation moves in that they need to start with small moves, and any switch in direction needs to read clearly and to happen smoothly.

A major problem with lights on a stop-motion set is that they are usually left on all day, and the slightest flicker, or movement in the lamp, or a bulb blowing, can ruin a shot. Any change of colour intensity or brightness will immediately register between frames. As with the sets, the lighting rig has to take into account the access of the camera and animators, and particularly the need for bulbs to be changed.

Obviously lighting can affect a film in many ways but its main function is to let the audience see what the directors want them to see. However, with stop-motion, lighting can also help with the movement and with the spatiality of the sets. For example, there's little point in having highly sculpted and textured puppets if a barrage of front and fill lighting is going to flatten everything. The lighting should show off every contour of the puppets and the depth of the sets. Likewise the movement of the puppets will be emphasised if there are shadows or dappled lighting for them to move through. To achieve this you should work closely with the lighting crew to plot the movement of any characters in a scene. Remember that texture and detail can be enormously effective in adding credibility to a film, but they are easily lost if they are completely hidden in shadow.

The Owl House 2008

animator
Jess Cope

The harsh reality of a set transformed into something living and credible, through all the elements of lighting, animation and detailed set dressing.

Crossfading is the technique of fading out one image or sound while simultaneously fading in a second image or sound.

Shadows

Like pauses in movement, shadows are an equally important part of lighting, giving drama and suspense, and a real sense of geography. For example, as most stop-motion takes place on table tops, with the lighting high above, it's all too easy to give the impression that none of our sets have ceilings. But, with a little planning, lighting can give the suggestion of an architecture that has not been built, or trees that aren't there, or a time of day, or warmth or cold. They can also help suggest a mood, much like colours.

Depending on the conscious artificiality of your plot, don't be frightened of using lighting as part of the storytelling, dimming or **crossfading** at the end of scenes, or highlighting areas in pools of light. Animation responds well to this theatricality.

Sound

Sound is too often treated as an afterthought, but it is a vital element of any film. As such it should be considered right at the beginning of the pre-production process along with all the other storytelling elements. As the stop-motion process doesn't allow us to record any live sound when filming, everything has to be created from scratch, and it can therefore be tempting to illustrate every step and every rustle of cloth.

You might be armed with a whole library of effects during the sound dubbing process, but these usually get slowly cut for being too heavy-handed or for simply cluttering up the visuals. The secret, as with everything in animation, is in being selective, and only using sound that helps the story or the atmosphere. Most cartoons use sound effects to highlight the comedy and energy in the squash and stretch movements with a barrage of slide whistles (or swanee whistles) and whooshes, but somehow the physicality of puppets doesn't always lend itself to such exaggeration.

Of course, this all depends on the tone of your film, and the extent to which your storytelling relies on sound. For example, consider whether the sound effect of a skid added to a shot of a character coming to a halt fits the action perfectly, or adds something extra to the energy of the character that wasn't there in the acting, or whether it is too big for the action.

It's also important to remember that an appropriate sound mix can help suggest the spatiality of the sets, and it is essential to have the voices balanced according to the geography of the characters. For example, in an extreme wide shot you are unlikely to hear the characters as clearly as in a close-up; likewise, you don't want a character at full volume in a close-up, and the recording of the voices needs to suggest this spatiality.

Lo Guarracino 2004

animator
Michelangelo Fornaro

Based on a Neapolitan tongue-
twisting song from the 18th
century of the same name,
Michelangelo Fonaro's gorgeous
short *Lo Guarracino* mixes
human actors and stop-motion
with tremendous wit. The artful
combination of the song,
stylised design and cabaret
style give an artifice that lets
the animation feel comfortable
alongside the live action.

Tip: Ambient sound

Ambient sound is extremely useful in
complementing the set and lighting
design. As with all these elements, try
not to always think of sound as a literal
reproduction of real life; sometimes the
most unlikely objects can provide the most
appropriate sound to a particular visual.
Most studios have libraries of effects, but
it's always more satisfying to create live
effects for the finished picture. The timing
works so much better when they are
created specifically for the animation.

As you plan your film, consider what
sounds will be required and experiment
with different means of creating those
sounds. Remember that silence can
also be very effective.

Music

Music can often seem a more natural partner to animation than dialogue. Animation is about movement, and music has movement within it. Also, the sublime artificiality of music seems to fit the artificiality of animation. For this reason, music should always be discussed at the start of planning a film.

You can use music simply as a background, to set the scene or help suggest the emotion. However, it can be so much more satisfying when it is used as part of the storytelling itself, with the music being conspicuously upfront as with a ballet. In this way, music can help push the animation away from a comfortable reality into something more interesting and exciting. If any scene requires a degree of choreography then you should ensure that you have access to the music ahead of filming. It is important to familiarise yourself with the nuances of the music well before you begin animating.

Tip: Rhythm

The music for my film *Next* drove the film forward, and was precisely worked out in terms of structure ahead of the filming; the beats giving me a guide to how many poses I needed to tell the story. I could have animated without the musical shape but I fear I would have easily wandered from the strict rhythm. We've seen how stop-motion needs to flow from one frame to another, from one shot to another. Music can help this enormously, giving a shape to what can sometimes be quite a fragmented process.

If you are having trouble with the pace and rhythm of your story, or a particular scene won't come together, try storyboarding it to synch up with some appropriate music. Remember that you will generally need permission to use someone else's music in your film.

Jason and the Argonauts
1963

animator
Ray Harryhausen

This skeleton battle is one of the most perfect sequences in the history of stop-motion. Bernard Herrmann's score celebrates the quirkiness of stop-motion while making it a thrilling action sequence. The instruments and percussive sounds chosen are so appropriate for the look and movement of the skeletons. Every element in this sequence works together to produce something no other technique could have managed.

There are so many ways of using music in your storytelling. One extreme is to have a full orchestra punctuate every action as in the glorious *Tom and Jerry* films, or you can use it more subtly as in Michaël Dudok de Wit's film *The Monk and the Fish* (1994) where the music sets the tone and delicately structures the film and movement. Many animators enjoy working with the discipline that a piece of music enforces, though it does not allow for improvisation or inspiration on the set (it is not usually possible to lengthen a piece of music to fit the action and so the action has to fit the music).

Highly artificial art forms, such as opera, lay out their communication conventions from the beginning. Even so, it sometimes jars to have an opera singer speaking naturalistic dialogue after a wildly elaborate aria, as the conflict between the two conventions is exposed and awkward. Similarly, animation is often set within fantastic worlds with strange perspectives and odd environments and peopled with gloriously bizarre characters. Naturalistic dialogue can sometimes sit uncomfortably in these settings as it can seem a shame to hamper extravagant creations with mundane dialogue. It's important to let the dialogue have the same stylistic freedom as the other elements of your film.

First, of course, you need to work out just how important the dialogue is in your film, and how much plot and character information it is revealing. Many animators are more comfortable using artificial forms of dialogue, such as singing or rhyme or even voice-overs. It's also worth remembering that most emotions can be conveyed through detailed body language, and this is certainly more animation friendly than a wealth of dialogue with minimal movement.

Most dialogue requires close-ups, and cutting back and forth between characters in a conversation; this definitely limits the movement potential of the characters and the film itself (although it is much simpler to film than more active scenes). Too often, especially in children's television, dialogue is a lazy way of telling what is happening rather than showing it.

Lip-synch

With dialogue comes the tricky issue of lip-synch, and many animators can get sidetracked with the pursuit of precise movement. Naturally, if the characters are speaking it will look odd if there is no movement of the mouth at all – the dialogue could be wrongly interpreted as narration. A lack of mouth movements can also make it difficult for the audience to easily understand who is speaking, unless the body language is clear. Of course, if the body language is completely clear then you may need to ask yourself if speech is necessary.

If you do choose to have dialogue, do ask yourself just how naturalistic you want it to be. If you are unable to match all the complex mouth shapes speech needs it's wiser to be more stylised (a simple mouth that can open and close is often effective if you concentrate on the rhythm). To be absolutely accurate, speech needs teeth, a tongue and a very pliable pair of lips, but most puppets simply don't have that detail, especially when the characters are animals who do not possess the mechanics for speech. Animating the intricate movements of a tongue inside a mouth is physically awkward and much easier for CG artists.

Animation can be so much more than it is usually allowed to be.

Henry Selick

▲

Coraline 2009

director
Henry Selick

The *Coraline* team developed a very elaborate use of replacements, rather than internal mechanics, for some stunningly precise lip-synch, with a surprising amount of nuance. The necessary resources to produce this effect are out of reach for most animators but the results are astonishing.

Tip: Avoiding lip-synch

There's no getting away from the fact that lip-synch slows the shooting process down with stop-motion, and also adds to the budget. Of course an unfortunate irony is that most children's programmes need dialogue, and subsequently sufficiently detailed mouth movements. These programmes are then sold abroad, needing the characters to be revoiced, making an absolute mockery of the original lip-synch. A popular solution to this problem is to invent an expressive, but universal language – as used by the ever mischievous Pingu the penguin. Regardless of the language being used, a certain amount of stylisation in the lip-synch is certainly the best way forward, but whatever convention you use, make sure that you introduce it to your audience straight away.

Sound > **Dialogue** > Special effects

Vocal performances

However you use dialogue, it is essential that it is recorded and broken down into frames on the **bar sheets** long before filming. An animator can fit loose mouth shapes to the dialogue much more easily than an actor can fit his or her voice to already filmed animation.

When recording the voices for stop-motion, the trick is to get as much physicality and spontaneity into the voices as possible, as well as an absolute awareness of the geography of the scene. Most animators will enjoy picking up on all the little breaths and pauses; seeing a puppet apparently stuttering over a word brings it to life. Anticipating a piece of dialogue by animating an intake of breath adds a surprising amount of life. Once again, it is the little unplanned imperfections that work so well.

A cold mechanical voice, treated almost as a voice-over, will not sit comfortably with the puppet. It is therefore vital to describe as best you can to the actor what the puppet will be doing; for example, are they running along a beach or whispering in a cupboard?

Any physical dynamics will only help the animation. It is important to encourage the actors to breathe life into the words with what they feel works, and where at all possible, it helps to have the cast for that scene in the same space looking at each other, so that the rhythm flows naturally. If this is not possible, have someone reading the lines off microphone so that you never have an actor performing their lines in isolation. Technically it's wise to leave a gap between each line of dialogue, but sometimes you can hear the actor anticipating that break so this should be treated on a case by case basis.

Of course, all this can mean that the animation performance has to, out of necessity, fit round the vocal performance. This can be inhibiting to the animation, therefore in an ideal world the animator will have some input with the voice work (such as suggesting certain bits of character business or physical actions that will affect the vocal performance). Try to make sure the dialogue and music is available on your work station as you shoot, so you can hear every accent and pause each frame. Refer to it as much as possible.

Tools and techniques

**Gilbert & Sullivan –
The Very Models** 1998

animator
Barry Purves

Mr Sullivan in full song. Though
he had no tongue and no teeth,
following the strong rhythm of
the music and versatile mouth
shapes made for convincing
lip-synch.

Shooting with digital technology has opened up almost unlimited possibilities for special effects. However, many stop-motion animators prefer to do as many effects as possible actually in the camera, on film, or on set. This analogue approach certainly gives the effects an integrity within the image, which the mixture of CG and a real set doesn't always manage. Low-budget CG often sits unhappily and flatly in a very spatial world. For example, it can be very difficult to convincingly insert a CG ball being thrown between two puppets. The CG artist must ensure that the lighting matches the scene, and introduce credible shadows. This may not be the most economical way of achieving the effect as the animator could easily suspend the ball on invisible thread on the set, and have the puppets properly interacting with the ball. A gentle knocking of the ball before the exposure provides a blur and hides the wires. Voila!

It is enormously satisfying to create these kinds of illusions in front of the camera, in the same space as the characters. This may be something of a Luddite view when technology can create such astonishing imagery, but it harks back to the origins of stop-motion with its simple tricks accomplished with nothing more than smoke and mirrors. There is also a naïve perception about the ease of CG imagery, which undermines the skill and ingenuity of the artists involved. This assumption that an effect is simple and somehow less impressive because a computer has been involved is entirely erroneous. However, many stop-motion animators still love getting their hands dirty. If you do, you'll probably be happy coming up with creative ideas on set.

The way that you use special effects will probably depend on the sophistication of your film, but try to use your imagination before immediately resorting to technology. It's more satisfying if you can control things on the set.

▶

Chicken Run 2000

directors
Peter Lord and **Nick Park**

Here we see the marvellous Ginger whiling away her time in a solitary confinement coal bin by bouncing a ball against the wall – echoing Steve McQueen's character in *The Great Escape* (1963). This was an interesting challenge for the animators.

Editors on stop-motion films have a hard job, as they can't do what editors usually do. On live-action films, and with CG to some extent, the editors are given an excess of footage (such as multiple angles of the same scene). They have plenty to play with and can therefore adjust the scenes in post-production to sharpen up the pace, or insert a close-up to help the storytelling, or even totally rearrange the order. Because of the time involved in creating stop-motion footage it is only practical to shoot what is deemed necessary. Occasionally, on a big set piece scene, it might make sense to have extra cameras shooting secondary detail. However, this can be difficult as there are often tricks (such as supports being hidden from the camera by the puppets' bodies) that would be exposed with a second camera.

So, how do we give editors a choice of shots? Generally, these choices have to be made on the storyboards during pre-production. This is a practical solution but bear in mind that things seldom go exactly to plan, and there are other ways to make the editor's job easier.

Spontaneity should be encouraged within the overall framework of your film, but it can make continuity difficult, especially if a film has been shot out of sequence. The unpredictability of stop-motion makes it difficult for action to flow into a previously filmed shot. If two shots don't match, the editor will need to disguise the lack of continuity by cutting away to an extra shot. Another common problem occurs when the time allocated for a particular shot is insufficient to act out the necessary action or highlight a particularly important prop.

In order to fix this problem the editor will need to add an unplanned close-up to help the flow of the story. Practically it helps if these changes are noticed by the director on the studio floor. Usually, by the time the editor is at work assembling the sequence, sets have been cleared away, or the scene has moved on, and it's not practical to go back for a **pick-up**.

All this has been made substantially easier with shooting on digital. Now shots can be enlarged, or the framing shifted a little, or characters may have been shot against a blue screen to allow them to be used again against a different background. A hold on an action can be extended or shortened if the timing wasn't quite right. Depending upon the economics of the film, a library of stock shots can be built up – this is certainly not ideal, but it is practical.

The animator can help give the editor flexibility by always shooting a few extra frames, even if it means overlapping some action. It's so easy for an animator, absorbed in the filming, to see the shot as a complete entity and bring things nicely to a halt – but the editor's job is to make every shot flow into the next smoothly. If two sequential shots have several frames of overlapping action, it will help the editor choose the right moment to cut, for general pacing or for synchronising with the dialogue or music.

It will always help the editor too, if the animator gives a good reason for a shot to be cut. Cutting to a close-up suggests something of interest is about to happen – it's even better if that something has already started to happen, motivating the cut.

Pick-ups are additional shots filmed after a sequence has been completed, due to some continuity error or a plot detail that requires more clarity.

▲

Paint on glass

animator
Caroline Leaf

Some techniques, such as
painting on glass, let the images
transform from close-up to long
shot, without the need for actual
cuts, producing a very lyrical and
continuous form of editing.

Tip: Leading into the next shot

Animators need to lead through into
the next shot by giving enough frames
of the incoming action. One or two frames
of a new movement are not enough as it
will just look like a twitch at the end of
the shot. There needs to be enough
movement, at least six frames, to let it
register as a movement. It may feel
awkward while shooting this on the set,
and look odd when you see the rushes,
but when the action is carried on into
the next shot the cut will be smooth
and invisible.

Special effects > **Editing**

Narrative flow

Editing must have seemed a strange and disorientating concept to the first film audiences, especially jumping from one location to another in consecutive frames, or from wide shot to close-up. This is not how the human eye works at all, so it is important that the images flow. Just as the animation of each frame must relate to the frame before and after in order to flow, so sequencing shots and cuts should also offer smooth transitions. For example, cutting from a wide shot with a character prominently on the right of frame to a close-up of the same figure on the left of frame will jar with the viewer. But if the figure is on the right of the wide shot and the close-up shot, then the transition is less awkward for the eye. It flows.

It isn't just the staging that needs to flow. The speed of a movement needs to match from one shot to another, which with stop-motion can be hard when shots have been filmed days apart and by different animators. Equally, if you cut from a brightly lit shot against a red background, to the same character shown from a different angle with a blue, shadowy background, then your scene just won't flow. Unless, of course, you want to create a disconnected feeling in your film, in which case this would be appropriate. Do remember, though, that animation struggles to flow at the best of times, so the more help we can give it using all the elements of film-making, the better. And this is where an editor can pull a film together.

Editors are removed from the blood, sweat and tears of the filming process and so are not precious about cutting or restructuring sequences – anything to make the storytelling work. Stop-motion shots tend to be shorter than with other forms of animation and film-making. This is because so many factors, such as running out of time, fatigue, a puppet falling over, the set wobbling or a light blowing, can cause a shot to go wrong. All this makes it very hard to sustain a lengthy shot. These difficulties are an inevitable consequence of the physical nature of stop-motion – they are also an exciting challenge. The effect, however, is that shots are not always the intended length, so that new shots have to be inserted.

Every cut causes a beat, and so it is important to be aware of any changes to the rhythm of a sequence that any new shots could cause. A film should move like music, with slow sequences, intercut with quicker sequences, with troughs and peaks, tensions and releases. The pace isn't just dependent on the action of the story; it is also dependent on the rhythm caused by alternating different sized shots, and lengths of shot, or changes of colour and sound. All of these elements affect the rhythm. Too much spontaneity on the studio floor and this essential rhythm might get lost. Editors can stand back and see the whole picture better than most.

Tomorrow 2009

animator
Bob Lee

This still uses bold lighting,
effective set and prop design,
dynamic composition and good
use of focus – all the elements
working together to produce a
very atmospheric frame.

Tip: Holding the shot

Editing can help the pace of any film with
the addition of quick cuts, but remember
that whereas a shot of just four frames of
blurred CG action can still be read by the
viewer, a four-frame shot of stop-motion
would be much harder to read. The lack of
blurring makes the illusion of movement a
little harder to maintain in stop-motion.
Also, the more different a shot is from its
predecessor, the longer the shift will take
to register with the viewer's brain.

Special effects > **Editing**

In this final chapter we will not only look at how to get clear readable animation, but also how to make it mean something. We'll look at the particular qualities and quirks of stop-motion, its unpredictability and its physicality, and how to make sure that every frame counts. We'll try to encourage inventive, imaginative animation, rather than straightforward literal animation. We'll look at how to give the illusion of elements such as weight and inertia, which help produce credible animation, and we'll stress the important aspects of performance, timing, and acting, essential to any movement.

◄

A Midsummer Night's Dream
1959

director
Jiří Trnka

Also known as *Sen noci svatojanske*, this beautiful award-winning film contains some outstanding performances. It was originally released without dialogue, telling the story through music, pantomime and dance. Later an English-language version used the voices of some of the great Shakespearean actors of the time, including narration by Richard Burton.

Tools and techniques > Movement and performance

Animating on the set

And so, with all the pre-production completed, you're ready to animate. This is the fun part, and this is really why we work in stop-motion. Remember that although the animation will seldom match the images in your head, with enough preparation and patience, it could be even better.

Hopefully on your set you will have at least a lighting cameraman, and someone, maybe the director, necessarily structuring your day. This will leave you to concentrate on the animation. How much you are expected to shoot every day is always down to budgets and the standard of animation required. Feature films often shoot a walk through and a final rehearsal, and then expect perhaps two to three seconds per day. This luxurious amount of time is made necessary by the high standard of animation required for a feature film (which will be exposed on huge screens). For television series work a daily rate can be between eight and 12 seconds. This is fast and doesn't allow for any rehearsal or retakes, which can be exciting. It's also quite hard and physical work but you can make it easier by being fully prepared and knowing exactly what you are doing when you start a shot. It's unlikely that you'll shoot every shot on a film, and even less likely that you'll shoot in sequence. It is therefore absolutely essential that you have a storyboard near you to check exactly how your shot fits in with the larger scheme of things and with the continuity. Also, check the puppet before each shot, testing that the tension of the joints will allow for easy movement.

If necessary stand in a quiet spot and act out the scene, just so you can internally feel the choreography of the action. Do not feel embarrassed, this will help you immeasurably. We are performers after all. Using a mirror to watch yourself perform the scene can be useful, but remember that it can be confusing if your puppet bears little resemblance to you. Most films will have the dialogue recorded before filming begins, so listen to this several times before you start. Try to catch the rhythm, breathing and accents of the actors. Animating little vocal tics, such as breaths or stutters, ties the voice closely to the puppet, and pleasantly surprises an audience.

Sometimes films have had two or more animators on a shot with numerous characters, but the communication necessary between the animators can slow the process down, and you may get several very different styles in one shot; you may also just get in each other's way. Most animators are happier by themselves, however much concentration it might require. This leads to a more satisfactory continuity of performance in the shot. If you can animate a whole sequence, then that's even better.

Prometheus Bound 2004

animator
Peter Dodd

Here we see a superbly animated writhing sequence that would have been very hard to emulate in stop-motion. To reproduce this in stop-motion would require a very subtly armatured spine and hips in the puppet, but the puppet being so close to the rock would have made access for a good grip and leverage difficult. Make sure that any scene you are planning is technically possible in your chosen medium.

Get comfortable

It is vital to make yourself comfortable at your set. Check that you can reach everywhere the puppet will walk, and that you can reach underneath the set for the magnets or tie downs. Also make sure that the camera and even the lights and reflecting boards won't get in the way of your access. It is also important to ensure that there is sufficient space to rest your elbows on a solid part of the set; this will ensure that your hands have good solid leverage. Without this resting place your arms are much more likely to wobble. Also, ask yourself whether you have got all the props or the replacements you need. How about tools? You will obviously need a monitor, a recording device, a soundtrack, the barsheets and the storyboards. Other, more easily forgotten tools include sticky gum, toothpicks and sharpened lollipop sticks (for reaching areas that fingers can't), Allen keys for tightening joints, pens for making marks on the monitor, a surface gauge, tweezers, a ruler to plan the space and the steps taken by the puppet, sculpting tools, masking tape and so on.

It will seem like a lot of clutter, but all of these tools will come in handy. Do also ensure that you can reach everything comfortably, and position the monitor within your eyeline when you are animating. Being forced to turn around from the set to look at the monitor is likely to disorientate you on each frame. It is important to avoid this in order to maintain some sort of muscle or spatial memory of the scene. Your time on the set will also be made easier if you can avoid treading over cables each frame, so clear the floor of any hazards – hazards to yourself or that could jeopardise anything happening on set. Consider whether the set is too cold or too warm and make what adjustments you can. If the floor seems hard or cold, do put some carpet down.

Stop-motion requires animators to spend long days on their feet, bending and stretching under the heat of the lights, and often in cramped conditions. These physical quirks are a serious consideration, especially when most other forms of animation let you sit in a comfortable chair for most of the day. For us, there's usually some backache along the way, and eye strain from focusing on objects so closely.

The shooting units are usually surrounded by black drapes, not just for lighting but also to help create a space where it is easy to focus. To add to this effect make sure that you put away anything that might break your concentration, as concentration is an essential part of the process. In other words... turn that phone off! These details may seem trivial, especially to drawn or computer animators (or film theorists) but they are a vital part of the stop-motion process.

Also, and this is outside of your control, but it is worth noting the importance of having flexible hands and fingers. Large chunky hands may not allow much fiddling about with tiny mechanics, so make sure that your puppet suits your ability to manipulate it.

Above all, before you click that first frame, be absolutely certain that you know exactly what the shot is about. Getting four hours into a shot and then discovering that your character is not holding a vital prop could be disastrous, and it is your responsibility to avoid this.

Movement and performance

▲

Chiodo Brothers set

An animator in action on a
Chiodo Brothers set, with
the monitor conveniently in
his eyeline.

Tip: Be prepared

Walk through the action in your head,
making marks or even pin figure drawings
on the barsheets for poses you need to hit
on certain cues. Having some sort of
barsheet, with the timing of the dialogue or
music all clearly broken down into frames,
is great discipline. Make subtle marks on
the set if necessary. Check that the
camera framing is wide enough to contain
all the action that you have planned.

Get started

Hold the puppet with one hand so that the main body is rock solid, and you are able to move the 'animatable' part with the other hand without affecting the rest of the body. This does take practice. It's essential that you use both hands in the process, as a casual one-hand technique will see the puppets wobbling. This is a constant challenge in stop-motion; everything needs to be solid and yet free to move.

When physically animating, judge an increment first by how the puppet feels in your hand, then see how that has translated to the screen. The screen is ultimately what counts, however be wary of concentrating on the screen rather than the puppet. As you move your puppet, try and find something to measure the move against, whether it is a detail in the background, or a shadow on the floor, or a mark on the monitor. It helps to have a visual, real or mental, record of how much you have moved so you can increase or decrease or replicate as necessary – a photographic and muscle memory are huge bonuses for stop-motion. Having the digital record is great, but having a mental record is even better.

Some animators watch the whole sequence after every frame taken to see how the movement builds up. Others prefer only to check the previous frame to see that the movements all relate – feeling the main movement through the puppet, and then refining or gently correcting it by looking at the last frame. Do what feels right for you, but ensure that you do not become disconnected from the puppet. This relationship is what stop-motion, and anything to do with puppets, is all about.

Checking the previous frame is also useful to see whether any lights have blown, or any props fallen over, or whether you have moved the camera. Most recording devices have an 'onion skin' option that allows you to see a transparent image of the previous frame superimposed on your current frame. This is perfect for directly comparing frames, and for seeing the increments. A physical mechanical gauge placed on the set with a pointer indicating a position on the character can help you judge a subsequent increment, as can drawing on the monitor screen. Good concentration and focus will also help, and try to keep to a routine of checking the various elements of the animation in sequence, then the lights, the camera move, and the set.

▶

Sunday Drive 2009

director
José Miguel Ribeiro

Here we see animator Marike Verbiest as she reaches in to animate on the set of José Miguel Ribeiro's *Sunday Drive*. Access for the animators often has to be cleverly disguised.

Movement and performance

Puppet design and movement

As we saw in Chapter 3, the anatomy of your puppet will affect the way it moves. Big feet, for example, will lead to a comedy walk with the knees having to be lifted high to flick the feet through. Conversely, if your puppet has short legs it will have a tiny fussy stride. With other forms of animation it is sometimes acceptable to cheat by allowing for a movement that defies the anatomy. Drawn characters, particularly, can stretch and squash as necessary. With puppets, and again this is part of their appeal, you are dealing with fixed limbs. Some characters can be given replacement limbs when they are needed for particular shots, but this can break the integrity of the puppet's physicality. Using, overcoming, and playing with this physicality is part of stop-motion's appeal.

The extent to which one can stretch a solid character depends on the material and on the tone of the film. Plasticine allows a certain amount of flexibility but, for example, the audience might not accept Aardman's Wallace or Gromit elongating as they run around a corner, as Tom or Jerry might have done. Whatever your puppet's limitations, the conventions of the character's moves have to be set up immediately in a film, and only broken after very careful thought.

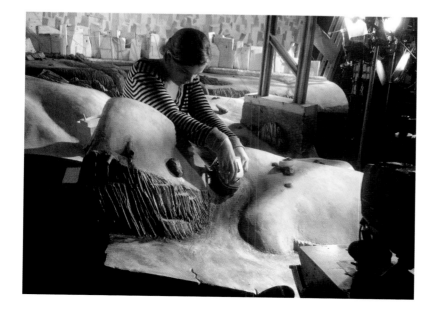

Animation needn't necessarily move with the smoothness of ballet, or reflect real life, as long as the audience can read the intention behind every frame of the movement. Jerky animation can work well if it comes across as deliberate. Good animation is about controlling and guiding the movement so that the significance, the emotion and the storytelling are understood with absolute clarity.

The technique and mechanics of stop-motion filming cannot ever reproduce an exact copy of live movement. A puppet will always have its own distinct way of moving. Whether this is attractive or not is another matter, but it's not something we should apologise for. Instead we should revel in its quirkiness.

Much live-action movement is too subtle, too complex, too fussy, and too erratic to be replicated in just 25 unblurred frames per second of animation. In live action, characters can move during the exposed frame; the resulting blurring gives the eye sufficient information about the direction of movement. With stop-motion, although complicated rigs can move a puppet during exposure, our characters are usually static in each frame, which makes a huge and crucial difference.

Stop-motion is about giving the idea of movement, the illusion of it, through being selective. However sophisticated the armature on your puppet, you simply will not be able to reproduce all the movements, all the strange little tics that happen in live action. It would be foolish to try. A puppet has limitations; it has a mechanical skeleton, which usually has far fewer joints than its human or animal equivalent and it must contend with the force of gravity.

These 'limitations' will be a drawback only if you are trying to reproduce reality, but they should really be liberating. In stop-motion, we have the freedom to produce movement that borders on dance, as we are expressing so much through our characters' body language. Stop-motion can still be subtle, but we have to enjoy the artificiality of the movement, and relish it. It's a waste to reproduce what live action does when puppets can be more florid or more mannered or more characterful or simply more static.

[On *Mary & Max*] the rule was that there would be no straight lines, no perfect circles, everything had to be a bit flawed because the script is about flawed characters.

Adam Elliot

Mary & Max 2009

animator
Adam Elliot

A heartbreaking still from *Mary & Max*. Adam Elliot's feature film revels in the low-tech, hands-on qualities of stop-motion.

Tip: Dynamics

It is vital to give the audience as much information as possible about the movement, height, and weight of the character as well as how it reacts to the environment, and why it is doing what it is doing. It's also important to balance strong, open and excessive movements, with moments of calm and stillness – stillness is an essential part of movement. This variation of dynamics gives so much life to characters.

For example, if a character is suddenly stopped by hitting a brick wall (in reality a harmless balsa wood or plaster construction), you can imply the solidity of the brick wall, or the characters' momentum, by the way in which the character bounces back with a judder. If it was a soft wall, you can imply the energy being cushioned by the wall. Without these real-world dynamics your character may simply look like a puppet in a set.

Enjoying movement

To enjoy stop-motion it helps to enjoy movement. Animation is a very physical medium and studying such activities as dance, mime, and sport, where the body is expressive and often in extreme poses can help animators enormously. Try to think like a dancer who, stuck with a very rigid anatomy, attempts to amaze the audience by seemingly crossing the line of what is physically possible. Animators, with puppets, are much the same. A puppet's movement is much more impressive when it flirts with its limits. But if it blatantly crosses these limits, defying gravity, defying anatomy, then it becomes very much less credible.

Experienced dancers have the ability, after suitable rehearsal, to dance through muscle memory, without having to consciously think through the moves. It flows naturally with one move leading to the next, directed by the music. While you won't always have the luxury of rehearsals, it should be possible to manage something similar by being very familiar with the storyboards, except your role is both that of a dancer and choreographer.

Tip: Snap to it

Many techniques from the world of dance can be used in stop-motion, as long as they are properly adapted. For example, dancers often 'pop' or 'snap' into a strong pose to accent it. This energetic flick is hard to translate directly into stop-motion as it would simply require too many frames, and it could easily look like an awkward jolt. However, it is possible to play with changes of rhythm that give the same effect. In dance this movement works by suddenly stopping and seemingly ignoring the physical rules of inertia. With stop-motion, it is almost the opposite. A puppet's movement works when the audience sees it affected by gravity, weight and inertia, as long as the effects are expressed clearly and deliberately.

The Birth of the Robot 1936

director
Len Lye

In this extraordinary commercial a man dies after driving into the middle of the desert but, with the help of Shell Mex oil, is reconstructed as the company's trademark robot. With simple, beautiful puppets, and Holst's *The Planets* condensed down to just seven minutes, this is a wonderful marriage of music, storytelling and imagination.

Movement and performance

Dancers do exactly what we do; they tell stories and reveal characters and thoughts through movement. Watching, and if possible taking part in, dance is invaluable in learning the potential and limitations of the human body. It is so helpful to be truly conscious of what your body is doing, how the weight is shifting, how it is balanced, and the shapes you are making. This awareness will help you 'see' movement, as it is not always easy to sketch stop-motion movements beforehand.

Sometimes schedules and budgets allow for a walk through, to check the positioning and the lighting; this simply requires animating the characters on approximately five frame poses. However, this is a luxury. Usually you will have to go straight into a take, and it certainly helps if you can visualise the shapes and movements of the characters, whether you have acted them out physically or internally.

Musical metaphors

Strong poses are an essential part of animation, just as they are vital for dance and sculpture. However, the length of time you keep a puppet in such a pose is a fine balance. Don't waste a lovely shape by only letting the viewer see it for a single frame; ease into it, hold it, and ease out of it. If you hold a pose for a long time, a puppet can still be communicating even through not moving. The trick is not to let the puppet suddenly die, with everything stopping on exactly the same frame. Some gentle secondary movement flowing and overlapping through the pause will keep the puppet alive. As silence is an integral part of music, so stillness is a part of movement; with music

we hear a note fade naturally and movement comes to a halt naturally. To suddenly stop a movement would be like a bad edit in music.

Keeping with the musical metaphor, just as single notes mean very little until they are put next to another note, so it is with gestures, and even individual frames. It is very helpful to think beyond the actual frame you are animating. Imagine how it fits within a larger phrasing of the movement. If you think of movement as no more than a series of individual frames somehow magically put together to produce some greater movement, it just won't work. You need to see the architecture of the whole gesture

and action. This is all about making movements flow into each other, by relating each frame to the previous one, and having in your head the much larger shape. A frame is only the single key on the piano, or using another appropriate metaphor, that of writing, a single letter. A full stop very clearly indicates the end of a thought or statement, or gesture, but a comma will link two thoughts or ideas into a single arc. Get away from the idea of thinking about individual frames and think about the scene and story as a whole.

A very good trick to help the flow and the overall shape of a move is to imagine a marker on any given point of a puppet: the end of a finger, or the chest, or knee joint. As you move through a shot, mark each frame, and if the line traced is clear, with a definite smooth shape, whether it be a constant forward line or a series of gentle curves, you can guarantee that it will be good animation. If the line is zigzagging erratically, the animation will be much less effective.

The right angle

dancer
David P. France

In the first shot (far left) the camera just misses the strength of the pose from this particular angle, though there are still some interesting shapes. In the second shot (centre) the legs have clarity but the arms don't read quite as well. In the third photo (left) every element of the body reads perfectly for the camera. As with animators, a dancer has to make sure that his body shapes are seen by the audience from the best angle.

How much potential for movement is there in your film? In stop-motion, movement is not just confined to the way a character moves. The way in which an environment reacts to a puppet can also often help to suggest movement. For example, as a character rushes through the frame, a disturbance of leaves or debris on the floor, or banging doors, can all help the illusion. Long scarves and bits of costumes trailing behind the character create the idea of movement. A movement is also more noticeable if there is background detail to move against. A puppet of a colour similar to its bland background, moving through flat, shadowless lighting, will not be as effective as a puppet standing out from its background moving through shadows. Movement in a sideways plane obviously registers more strongly than a movement towards the camera, but that sideways movement doesn't make the most of the real space that is one of the great advantages stop-motion has over other forms of animation. Placing objects in the foreground, so that characters can move behind them, creates huge depth. Similarly, the choice of lenses can help accentuate a movement and depth. Close-up lenses tend to squash and flatten the space while wide-angle lenses make a small space look bigger, with any movement towards the camera having more dynamics, making the depth of the space more noticeable.

Speed

Every movement can benefit from a change of speed. It is therefore important to understand that fast movement comes from widely spaced increments, and slower movements from narrowly spaced increments. For example, a movement that is accelerating will have gradually increasing increments. It might help you to visualise this by drawing a movement as drawn animators do, seeing how the increments cluster for the slow start of the action and then spread out for the fast bit.

As you are developing your animation try to find the dynamics in every action, the changes of rhythm and accent. This can be hard to coordinate, especially if there are several characters, or parts of characters, all moving at different speeds. You will need to remember and coordinate all the different tempos, just like a conductor or a choreographer. New animators sometimes try to simplify the movement of the various different limbs by creating symmetry in the poses (this is also known as twinning). Unless it is used as a conscious part of the storytelling, this can look very lazy and uninteresting. Even though animating two limbs doing different things is harder to remember it is well worth the effort as energetic movements in one hand can be balanced by more measured movements in the other.

War Horse

director
**Marianne Elliott
and Tom Morris**

In this powerful National Theatre production each horse is beautifully performed by three very visible operators. This shares much with stop-motion, where the audience are complicit with the technique of bringing the characters to life, and that is an essential part of the storytelling. It is more rewarding than a literal approach.

Being less literal

Sometimes a gesture, such as a subtle tut with a raised eyebrow, will require so many frames to mechanically spell out the action that the timing becomes laboured and the meaning is lost. In this case you need to find other ways to portray the same meaning, such as a slight sigh. Likewise, if your character must push a button, the actual button may not move or it might be too fiddly to manipulate. This will require you to emphasise the action in other ways, such as making more of the wrist pushing the hand, and more of the actual release. A character banging away on a piano keyboard may not have the dexterity in its fingers to accurately spell the notes out, so a more conscious emphasis on the rhythm of the hands would work. None of this is necessarily realistic, but in stop-motion the realistic way is seldom the most appropriate, the most expressive or the most readable.

As animators, everything we do from the narrative to the movement itself is an illusion, and we have to find the clearest, most direct way of creating this illusion. For example, a small puppet representing a full-scale human weighs very little, so to animate it landing after a jump, we need to give the illusion of a much larger and heavier character. This could be done by emphasising the compression in the knees and body, and letting the arms swing down heavily; by taking a few more frames to spell out the action. This immediately takes the timing away from live action, but it does tell the story clearly. However, as with the 'tut' above, too many frames can make the gesture less effective.

Always ask how fast something should move, and the answer should be dictated not by the size of the puppet in front of you but by the imagined weight and scale of the character, its anatomy and its emotion. If the character is meant to be the size of a house it will probably move with smaller, slower increments than something meant to be the size of a small cat. The speed of the character immediately suggests its weight. And emotionally, a melancholy character is unlikely to move as fast as a character delirious with joy. Keep questioning yourself about how and why a character will move. How can you represent the character's emotions through movement? Don't take the easy route of having a character saying that they are happy. Instead show that they are happy. For example, children's programmes very often finish with all the characters laughing – sometimes the puppets don't have moving mouths and so have to laugh with their whole body in a staccato rhythm. This less literal approach is how you need to start to think. It's far more imaginative.

Judder 2008

animator
Emily Baxter

Even a puppet without fully moving features can still express a thought process with good body language. Here a character from Emily Baxter's *Judder* certainly looks deep in thought.

Coppélia

production
Birmingham Royal Ballet

Here Swanhilda pretends to be the doll Coppélia. Her rigid angular shapes and lack of natural fluidity instantly suggests something mechanical. Notice her unfocused eyes, implying the lack of any thought process. *Coppélia* plays with many fascinating ideas and variations about giving the inanimate life.

Lively movement > **Helping the movement** > Performance

Show the mechanics

Every action is made up of several pieces of action, and it's important that the mechanics of what is happening are seen. Just the action of a character rising from a sitting position has to include a moment when the character makes the decision, the thought process, to rise. This is the start of the movement – in the eyes, and then the head. Then the viewer needs to see the weight transferred from the character's bottom to over his feet planted solidly on the ground, which involves the torso leaning forwards and the backside balanced backwards. Then the backside has to be pushed under the torso, as the torso straightens up, with the head finally coming to rest on the shoulders. This is the end of the movement. All this happens in a few frames in live action, but it helps to create a credible movement if we linger over the storytelling moments and changes of direction, enjoying the curves inherent in the action. You don't have to stop at the key moments but highlighting them lets the action read. Make sure you can find these moments in every action, and see where the movement starts and finishes.

Again, movement is so often like a piece of music. A single sustained note, like a single smooth continuous movement, is dull. But if you start to add rhythms and accents, and different pacing, it will become very much more interesting. Fortunately with stop-motion, it is quite hard to provide a single sustained movement. Human error leads to irregular increments. Computer animators have to learn to give these increments rhythm and dynamics, and stop-motion animators have to use the irregular increments and turn them into something deliberate.

Jumping is a complicated movement in any form of animation; it requires every part of the process to be shown clearly. However, in stop-motion it is a particularly tricky move. There are a variety of ways to achieve it. Stop-motion puppets, by their very nature, make good solid contact with the floor. This is usually an advantage but sometimes it is hard to make them look light on their feet. Standing on tip-toes takes subtle and strong mechanics in the feet joints and possibly a suspending string, and good balance. Having puppets go even further and actually jump is even more complicated but well worth the effort. To animate a run without the puppet leaving the ground can look clunky, but to suspend a puppet takes time and inevitable post-production work.

If you are shooting on film then sometimes the suspending wires can be hidden, but the sharpness of digital exposes such wires. On the other hand, if you are shooting digitally this will allow the use of rigs that can be edited out afterwards – although this costs both time and money, if you aren't able to do it yourself. This needs to be carefully thought through on the set, as it requires a still image (a plate) of the empty shot, enabling detail to be replaced in the image where the rigs had been. It never hurts to take an empty image of the beginning of the shot and at the end to help any corrections needed in post-production. A camera move complicates it even further as you may need to film the camera move without characters so you have all the detail from every angle covered.

A simple rig

animator
Chris Walsh

Here we see a simple but inventive rig that, when suitably framed, allows a puppet to appear to be jumping off the ground. This character is from Chris Walsh's *The Magic Projector*.

Tip: Let it read

One of the most important lessons of stop-motion is that every gesture should 'read'. You can ensure this happens through the clarity of the pose and by ensuring you include enough meaningful frames to tell the story and show the mechanics. For example, in live action an object or character might change direction in the exposure of a single frame. To achieve the same effect in stop-motion we need to spell it out for the viewer. We must show the object slowing down, the change of direction, and then speeding up again. Really show the effect of inertia on the object, angling it as it changes direction. If something is going to be done, make sure it is done clearly. Likewise, if something is not moving, let it sit there without twitching, and give the viewer time to realise it is sat there deliberately. One frame does not make a pause.

Lively movement > **Helping the movement** > Performance

There is nothing mystical about performance. At its most basic, it is about letting every controlled movement, every angle of the head, every change of rhythm, every pause, every walk and every blink express and reveal something about the character or the narrative. It is about presentation. It is about using the blink of an eye, not just to serve as a biological function but to show a thought process.

All of this takes a thorough understanding of body language. And do be aware that body language is not always universal. Many gestures come from specific cultural references, or learned and coded roots, but others are pure logical mime. For example, a single raised finger has many widely different interpretations around the world. It is therefore important to use open and honest forms of gestures and body language; movements and shapes that, though not literal, are completely clear in their meaning and emotion. Once you find exactly the movements that can define characteristics such as anger or yearning, you can apply that just as well to a household object as to a fully articulated puppet; there may be several defining movements but try to combine them into one clear, precise, and preferably understated movement. The less clutter the better.

In any language the order of the units of vocabulary and the ways in which they are combined are of prime importance, as are the inflections and rhythms. Body language is no exception; it needs punctuation and grammar to separate or complement each gesture. Rather than words you will be working with a whole complex lexicon of gestures, poses, attitudes and airs. The different combinations can produce unlimited meanings. Give each character his or her own clearly defined repertoire of gestures before you start filming, and keep to these. It will help to define them.

Usually animation is not reliant on a vocal language and you will have the freedom to over-emphasise and to enjoy body language, making the most of moments of action and stillness, of weight and lightness.

Casting

In much the same way that actors are cast in particular roles, animators are often cast for particular qualities. Of course, some animators are equally at home in all types of scenarios, but you'll find that some are much better at slapstick, while some are better at the quieter character-driven scenes. A good director will recognise this and give animators appropriate scenes. It will certainly serve you to practise as many different emotions and styles as possible. Stop-motion not only demands that you become an actor, it also asks that you play a very wide range of characters and interpret some very strange tales. In addition to human characters, you will be asked to perform monsters, inanimate objects, fantasy characters, totally abstract ideas and characters that don't have any recognisable means of communicating human emotions.

However, at the heart of most animation will be a clear human characteristic – in the world of animation even vegetables, cute animals and monsters have emotions and desires and frustrations and goals. Your huge challenge is to make such things seem credible and natural, and tell stories that the viewer will identify with. You need to be able to see the fable in every situation and character.

(R)evolution 2001

animator
Michael Cusack

Working out the body language for such stylised creatures must have been very exciting. Depriving characters of easily expressive arms and legs forces the animator to be creative. The easy route is not always the more interesting.

Exercise: Reconstruction

Take a few seconds of an iconic live-action scene from a film, and reconstruct it with very basic household objects, analysing exactly what it is about the performance, the movement and the drama that make it work. Hone it down to just the key moments, such as a certain tilt of the head or a tentative step or the well-timed look over the shoulder. Go directly to the heart of the scene. An animator should be able to look at any movement and find the storytelling part of it.

Helping the movement > **Performance**

Timing

When you have been animating in the studio for an hour on an action that may only be a couple of seconds of screen time, it is all too easy to think that the filmed action feels long. Try always to think in terms of the timing in the world on screen, and not in the studio; and don't confuse the two. It is surprisingly difficult to separate these two time scales, but it does get easier with experience.

New animators find it particularly hard to give a held action, or pause, enough time to register with the viewer. Instead, they often rush on to the next action, killing the moment and ruining the pose. To avoid this, you just need to give the audience sufficient time to see the physical mechanics of a movement or, again, the thought process and reactions involved in a piece of acting.

When you are animating the reactions of a character to a loud bang, for example, it's tempting to have the character jump back the very next frame, but that would deny the thought process, and ruin the credibility. If you wait a few frames and see the face register before the body reacts, there's more of a credible story. Don't be frightened of explaining a movement in too great a detail for your audience. One clear gesture, which has time to breathe, is better than several that are rushed. Timing is no mystery; it is just about showing the thought process and the mechanics.

Walking

As we saw in Chapter 3, your puppet should combine practicality with interesting design, and have sufficiently long and accessible legs to allow the character to walk if necessary. Ideally you need to hold the torso rigidly with one hand, while manipulating the legs with the other. This is where a third hand would be ideal. It's essential to make sure that the torso is moving forward in each frame as it can easily get knocked about. It's therefore worth tracing the progress of the torso, and every limb, by marking it off on the screen, making

▶

The Typewriter 2004

animator
Richard Haynes

Here we see movement guides from Richard Haynes' short film *The Typewriter*. Most animation techniques allow for some refinement during the process. With stop-motion we have no real equivalent of visualising a movement in advance, and have to get it right first time.

Movement and performance

sure the increments are going in the right direction. But, as with most actions, it's important to understand what defines the motion. The inverted V of a walk, as the back foot peels off the floor and the front foot slaps down, is the strongest shape in a walk and needs to be emphasised. Don't rush through this moment. The poses of the back leg flicking through tell less of a story than the key pose. Look at the rhythm of a person walking, watch the rise and fall; it's all too easy to get over complicated and lose this.

In live action, the subtleties of a walk are immense, but you are unlikely to have the puppet, the patience, or the time to accurately copy these, and nor should you. Once again, it's about selection and animating only what is essential and that defines the action. A march, for example, uses sharp, rigid limbs with very little softening at the end of moves, whereas a walk will see the relaxed arms following through with a slight delay. As is so often the case with stop-motion, when making your puppet walk, you should aim to make it credible rather than realistic.

rough animation

clean-up

trace

final

Helping the movement > **Performance**

▲

Brambly Hedge 1996

production
Cosgrove Hall Films

The anatomy of these beautiful puppets meant that they had to balance on their toes most of the time. Here the feet were tied to the set. There were invariably many characters acting in a scene with a combination of mouse and human behaviour – and all those tails. This created extra work, but effective expression.

Movement and performance

Animal movement

Four-legged creatures are always a challenge, not just for the sheer complexity of working out the choreography of each leg, and their different stages of locomotion, but also for trying to get access to each of the legs. A four-legged character is much more 'closed' than a character on two legs and this certainly complicates the animation process. Likewise, there's double the amount of securing to the set than with a biped.

Therefore, if you have animal characters in your film you must decide very early on how they will move and communicate. If you choose to keep an animal character on all fours, you are losing a certain amount of expression in the limbs, which will be needed for locomotion. This means you'll need to convey all the expression through the head and tail, assuming your animal has one (tails and ears are a vital part of communication in animal characters). Alternatively, if you put them on two legs, you lose a certain amount of natural animal behaviour but gain much recognisable human behaviour.

It's interesting to see how, even in the flexible world of animation, some animated animals lend themselves to becoming two-legged versions and some clearly don't. It often seems that relatively small animal characters, such as Mr Toad from *The Wind in the Willows* or the *Brambly Hedge* mice easily adapt to two legs while larger quadrupeds such as giraffes and elephants only look comfortable on four legs. Perhaps it is about size. Perhaps it is about freeing the movement from the restraints of realistic behaviour and celebrating movement as a result of expression rather than anatomy.

Exercise: Anthropomorphism

In stop-motion animating animal movement is rarely about recreating actual animal movement. Instead, it is more often about creating human movement within the loose parameters of animal anatomy. Anthropomorphism is still a huge part of what every animator faces each day.

Choose a friend or relative and try to imagine what animal they most resemble. Ask them to strike an appropriate pose and then find a clear line, shape and story in that pose. It should then be possible to translate the pose into a rough sketch of the appropriate animal. It doesn't need to be beautifully drawn; it just needs to catch the energy and character of the pose in animal form. If you find it easy to translate a human model into a giraffe, for example, then you are certainly an animator. It is what we do, and it's certainly an exciting challenge.

The need for patience is brought up every time stop-motion is mentioned, and it is true that stop-motion animators need patience. That doesn't just mean being calm. It means unreservedly accepting that the process is laborious, tedious, ridiculously fussy, stupidly slow, and will require a huge amount of effort for a relatively small effect. Accepting this can be challenging, and many people who begin working in stop-motion ultimately find easier ways to make films.

However, if you find pleasure in the minutiae of the craft, or shiver with excitement at the resonances of a puppet seemingly moving by itself; then you may soon be hooked. If you can appreciate that the few seconds of film produced in a day is an achievement, then welcome to stop-motion. You will find huge satisfaction in the sheer painstaking fiddliness of the craft, from getting your hands dirty, from trying to control the smallest detail, and even from the sheer repetition of the process. If you want to bring extraordinary and very credible characters to life through the intimate contact of your hands, then stop-motion is certainly for you.

You'll need an acceptance that the unpredictable will happen. See this as a positive quality, and don't see it as your film changing but as your film growing. Once you accept this, stop-motion really can be addictive, as you have made something seemingly move by itself; in effect, created some life. People who have never tried it can sometimes find this need to give things life, this compulsion to tell stories, hard to comprehend, and perhaps that is what gives it a special appeal. Maybe we do feel a bit of an exclusive smugness and pride after a rather exciting piece of animation, when what is obviously a piece of cloth and metal has credibly acted out some scenario or emotion and made someone laugh or cry – and we've done it with just our hands.

Stop-motion certainly does require a particular way of looking at things (not everyone is capable of looking at an inanimate object and seeing a character or an inherently dramatic situation). Not everyone can look at a simple object and ask 'what if?' The rewards are just as particular, but it is something that you have to love doing, otherwise something very special can seem a lot of sound and fury signifying nothing.

More than 30 years on, I still love every frame. I'm sure you will too.

A unique relationship

Giordano Ferrari (left) contemplates a puppet head in his likeness, while the marionette Doreen (far left) contemplates her own hand puppet. The relationship between puppet and puppeteer is quite unique, with both supplying equal parts of the performance.

A brief history of stop-motion

1896 Film-maker and showman Georges Méliès develops many of the tricks still used in stop-motion, especially substitution by stopping the camera.

1899 Arthur Melbourne Cooper animates matches for *Matches: An Appeal*. This was the first commercial to use stop-motion.

1900 In *The Enchanted Drawing*, J. Stuart Blackton mixed drawn animation and objects.

1907 Edwin S. Porter brings dolls and teddies to life in *The Teddy Bears*.

1910 *The Battle of the Stag Beetles* was the first of Ladislaw Starewicz's stop-motion films to produce detailed performances from insect and animal characters.

1915 Willis O'Brien makes a short film about a caveman and a brontosaurus, entitled *The Dinosaur and the Missing Link: A Prehistoric Tragedy*, just a year after Winsor McCay's *Gertie the Dinosaur* first appears.

1923 Buster Keaton's *Three Ages* features a short animated sequence with Keaton on a dinosaur.

1925 *The Lost World* sees Willis O'Brien's dinosaurs appearing on screen with real actors.

1926 Lotte Reiniger's *The Adventures of Prince Achmed* used delicate and complex cut-out silhouettes.

1930 Starewicz makes the feature *The Tale of the Fox* (also known as *Le Roman de Renard*), one of the few early animations to follow a darkly comic storyline.

1933 *King Kong* is released, with astonishing animation by Willis O'Brien.

1935 *The New Gulliver* (also known as *Novyy Gulliver*), directed by Aleksandr Ptushko, features a live actor and 3,000 animated puppets.

1942 The George Pál film *Tulips Shall Grow* features dozens of goose-stepping characters animated through replacement puppets.

1949 Jiří Trnka makes the feature-length *The Emperor's Nightingale* (also known as *Císaruv slavík*). The American dub is narrated by Boris Karloff.

1952 Norman McLaren films *Neighbours* through pixilation, animating humans as if puppets.

1953 Ray Harryhausen supplies the effects for his first major feature film, *The Beast from 20,000 Fathoms*.

1954 Michael Myerberg and John Paul retell the story of *Hansel and Gretel*, based on the opera by Engelbert Humperdinck.

1955 Gumby, a clay animation character created by Art Clokey, is introduced on US television.

1958 George Pál's *Tom Thumb* mixes animated puppets with actors.

1959 Jiří Trnka makes a spectacular puppet version of *A Midsummer Night's Dream* (also known as *Sen noci svatojánské*).

1963 *Jason and the Argonauts* is released with the classic skeleton battle sequence, animated by Ray Harryhausen.

1965 Jiří Trnka's political film *The Hand* is released.

1970 *Dougal and the Blue Cat* (or *Pollux et le chat bleu*), a feature film, is released, based on the TV series *The Magic Roundabout* by Serge Danot.

1974 Britain falls in love with *Bagpuss*, a children's television show by Peter Firmin and Oliver Postgate, who also gave the world *The Clangers*, *Noggin the Nog* and *Pogles Wood*.

1975 Ivo Caprino animates the hugely popular *The Pinchcliffe Grand Prix* (also known as *Flåklypa Grand Prix*).

1975 Industrial Light & Magic is formed, producing extraordinary special effects for features, with Phil Tippett being responsible for stop-motion in such films as *The Empire Strikes Back* (1980).

1976 Caroline Leaf animates coloured oil on glass for *The Street*, followed the year after by Kafka's *Metamorphosis of Mr Samsa* animated in sand.

1977 *Morph*, created by Dave Sproxton and Peter Lord of Aardman Animations, makes his first appearance on British television.

1977 Co Hoedeman wins an Oscar for his short film *The Sand Castle* (*Le Château de sable*).

1979 Yuri Norstein makes *Tale of Tales* (*Skazka skazok*), which is often cited as the greatest animation short.

1981 *Clash of the Titans* was released; this was the last major film for which Ray Harryhausen contributed animated characters.

1982 Jan Švankmajer makes *Dimensions of Dialogue* (*Moznosti dialogu*) and Tim Burton makes his short film *Vincent*.

Early 1980s Video playbacks appear in studios, enabling animators to see the previous frame, and a sequence as it is filmed.

1983 British animation studio Cosgrove Hall begin their adaptation of Kenneth Grahame's *The Wind in the Willows*. They will produce many iconic stop-motion TV series, including *Postman Pat*.

1985–6 Will Vinton's studios make the clay animation feature *Mark Twain*, as well as creatures in *Return to Oz*.

1986 The Brothers Quay make their short film *Street of Crocodiles*.

1988 Jan Švankmajer makes *Alice* (*Něco z Alenky*), featuring both live action and stop-motion.

1989 Nick Park's short films *A Grand Day Out with Wallace and Gromit* and *Creature Comforts* are both released by Aardman Animations.

1992 *Shakespeare: The Animated Tales*, was a series of condensed animated adaptations of Shakespeare plays produced by a multinational collaboration, followed in 1995 by *Operavox*, six animated operas.

1992 Mackinnon and Saunders is formed in Manchester, creating stop-motion puppets for TV, features and commercials. Their first production is Barry Purves' *Rigoletto*.

1993 Tim Burton produces the stop-motion feature *The Nightmare Before Christmas*, directed by Henry Selick.

1999 Dave Borthwick directs the pixilated *The Secret Adventures of Tom Thumb*.

2000 Aardman releases its first feature film, *Chicken Run*, directed by Nick Park and Peter Lord.

2003 Adam Elliot wins the Oscar with his clay animation film *Harvie Krumpet*.

2005 Tim Burton's *The Corpse Bride* and *Wallace and Gromit: The Curse of the Were-Rabbit*, directed by Nick Park and Steve Box, are both released.

2007 Frédéric Guillaume and Samuel Guillaume release *Max & Co*, a stop-motion feature film.

2008 Tatia Rosenthal's feature film *$9.99* is released.

2009 *Coraline*, directed by Henry Selick, released in 3D. Other stop-motion features released include Adam Elliot's *Mary and Max*, and Wes Anderson's *Fantastic Mr Fox*.

2010 *O Apóstolo* directed by Fernando Cortizo is released.

Conclusion > **A brief history of stop-motion** > Picture credits

P3 *Max & Co* courtesy of Frédéric Guillaume and Samuel Guillaume, 2007. © Cinemagination
P7 *She-Bop* courtesy of Joanna Priestley.
P8 *The Pigeon* courtesy of Hywel Prytherch Roberts.
P12 *Clash of the Titans* courtesy of MGM / The Kobal Collection.
P15 *Cinderella* courtesy of Melies / The Kobal Collection.
P17 *The Tale of the Fox* courtesy of Wladyslaw Starewicz Productions / The Kobal Collection.
P18 *Pas de Deux* National Film Board of Canada / The Kobal Collection.
P19 *Edgar Allan Poe* Courtesy of Alan Louis © Center for Puppetry Arts ®. Photography by Bill Jones.
P21 *Cityco Christmas Campaign 2009* courtesy of Loose Moose and Amaze.
P22 *Achilles*, a Bare Boards production for Channel Four television. Still by Paul Stewart. Directed by Barry Purves and produced by Glenn Holberton.
P24 Stage puppets courtesy of Blind Summit Theatre / Nick Barnes and Mark Down.
P25; 54; 107 *Next* – An Aardman Animations film, stills by Dave Alex Riddet, directed by Barry Purves, produced by Sara Mullock.
P27; 78; 87 *Rigoletto,* A Bare Boards production for S4C. Still by Mark Stewart. Directed by Barry Purves and produced by Glenn Holberton.
P28 *Puffer Girl* courtesy of Joan C. Gratz.
P29 *Wife of Bath (Canterbury Tales Part 1)* courtesy of Joanna Quinn.
P30 *The Wrong Trousers* © Aardman/Wallace and Gromit Ltd 1993.
P31; 53 *Harvie Krumpet* courtesy of Melodrama Pictures Pty Ltd.
P32; 75; 102; 128 *Gargoyle* courtesy of Michael Cusack and Anifex Pty Ltd. Photography by JoAnne Bouzianis-Sellick.
P33; 80; 186 *Billy Twinkle: Requiem for a Golden Boy* courtesy of Ronnie Burkett Theatre of Marionettes. Photography by Trudie Lee.
P34–35; 129; 159 *Tomorrow* courtesy of Bob Lee / Siobhan Fenton. Funded by 4mations Digital Shorts scheme © 2009.
P36 *King Kong* courtesy of Universal/Wing Nut Films / The Kobal Collection.
P37 *King Kong* courtesy of RKO / The Kobal Collection.
P39 *The Dam Busters* courtesy of Associated British / The Kobal Collection.

P41 *The Empire Strikes Back* courtesy of Lucasfilm / 20th Century Fox / The Kobal Collection.
P43 Test shot for Talos *Jason and the Argonauts* with thanks to Tony Dalton, courtesy of Ray and Diana Harryhausen Foundation.
P43 *Clash of the Titans* courtesy of MGM / The Kobal Collection.
P44–45 *$9.99* courtesy of Tatia Rosenthal / Sherman Pictures / Lama Films.
P46 *I Live in the Woods* courtesy of Max Winston.
P47 *The Pogles* courtesy of Loaf, The Dragons Friendly Society.
P48 *Christmas Dream* courtesy of Kratky Film / The Kobal Collection.
P50–51 *Damaged Goods* courtesy of Barnaby Barford, 2008. An Animate Projects commission for Channel 4 in association with Arts Council England.
P55 *The Nightmare Before Christmas* courtesy of Touchstone/Burton/Di Novi / The Kobal Collection.
P56; 96; 101 *Life's a Zoo* created by Adam Shaheen and Andrew Horne II. © 2008 Cuppa Coffee Studios.
P59 *Alice in Wonderland* courtesy of Lou Bunin Productions / The Kobal Collection / Limot.
P60; 151 *Coraline* courtesy of Focus Features / The Kobal Collection.
P62 *Street of Crocodiles* courtesy of Koninck Studios Ltd.
P63 *Animal Farm* courtesy of Vivien Halas. © The Halas & Batchelor Collection Limited.
P65 *Mary Poppins* courtesy of Walt Disney Pictures / The Kobal Collection.
P67 *Balance* courtesy of Christoph and Wolfgang Lauenstein.
P69 *Skhizein* courtesy of Jeremy Clapin / Dark Prince.
P70–71 *Creature Discomforts* courtesy of Leonard Cheshire Disability.
P73 *Babylon* © Channel Four Television 1986. © Aardman Animation.
P76 *There There* courtesy of Chris Hopewell © Collision Films.
P80 *The Tinderbox* courtesy of Purves Puppets. Reg's Revenge courtesy of Nat Miller.
P80; 147 *Lo Guarracino* courtesy of Michelangelo Fornaro.
P81 *All My Relations* courtesy of Joanna Priestley.
P82 *Corpse Bride* courtesy of Warner Bros. / The Kobal Collection.
P84; 104–105 *In the Fall of Gravity* courtesy of Ron Cole, Wobbly Tripod.

P85 *Screen Play*, a Channel Four / Bare Boards Productions. Directed, written and animated by Barry Purves. Produced by Glenn Holberton.
P86 *Jack the Giant Killer* courtesy of United Artists / The Kobal Collection.
P88 *The Family Story* courtesy of Chris Walsh.
P89 *Ami* courtesy of Dominique Bongers.
P90 *Small Birds Singing* courtesy of Linda McCarthy and Steven Appleby / Tiny Elephants Ltd.
P91; 94; 95; 118; 131; 140 *Friendly Fire* courtesy of Andy Kaiser/ The End of the Pier films.
P93 *The Dark Crystal* courtesy of Henson/Universal / The Kobal Collection.
P97 *The Astronomer's Sun* courtesy of Jessica Cope. ©UK Film Council and Screen Yorkshire.
P98 *Pingu* courtesy of HIT Entertainment Ltd and Joker INC d/b/a The Pygos Group.
P100 *Bob the Builder* courtesy of HIT Entertainment Ltd and Joker INC d/b/a The Pygos Group.
P101; 179 *The Magic Projector* courtesy of Chris Walsh.
P103; 130 *Madame Tutli-Putli* photographs used with permission of the National Film Board of Canada.
P106 *Tales from the Powder Room* courtesy of Darren Burgess and Anifex Pty Ltd.
P108 *Beaver Creek* courtesy of Ian Timothy © 2009.
P109 *Faust* courtesy of Heart Of Europe / Lumen / Athenor / The Kobal Collection.
P111 *Morph* © Aardman Animation 1980.
P113; 157 *The Owl who Married a Goose* courtesy of Caroline Leaf. A National Film Board of Canada Production.
P113 *Bear with Me* courtesy of Uriah Naeh, Bezalel Academy of Art and Design, Jerusalem.
P115 *Les Trois Inventeurs* courtesy of Michel Ocelot, Studio O. *The Tale of Sir Richard* courtesy of Peter Dodd.
P116; 169 *Mary and Max* courtesy of Melodrama Pictures Pty Ltd.
P120–121 *Mutt* courtesy of Glen Hunwick, Circe Films and Glen Art Productions.
P122; 123; 165 *Winter Break Tales* courtesy of Chiodo Bros Productions Inc.
P125 *Electreecity* courtesy of Sarah Davison and Sarah Duffield-Harding, UCA 2008.
P126–127 *Hide and Seek* courtesy of Kerry Drumm & Aaron Wood.
P132 *Lavatory Lovestory* courtesy of Konstantin Bronzit. © Melnitsa Animation Studio.
P133 *L'Oiseau* © Double Mètre Animation / Samuel Yal.

P134 *Wallace and Gromit: The Curse of the Were Rabbit* courtesy of Dreamworks/Aardman Animations / The Kobal Collection.
P137 *Les Triplettes de Belleville* courtesy of Sony Pictures Classics / The Kobal Collection.
P143 *Amelia Jane* courtesy of Lynne Pritchard, Gingermog.
P144–145 *The Owl House* courtesy of Jess Cope, The Edinburgh College of Art.
P149 Test for the skeleton sequence *Jason and the Argonauts* with thanks to Tony Dalton, courtesy of Ray and Diana Harryhausen Foundation.
P153 *Gilbert & Sullivan The Very Models* – A Bare Boards production for Channel Four Television. Directed by Barry Purves, produced by Christopher O'Hare. Still by Jean Marc Ferriere.
P154 *Chicken Run* courtesy of Dreamworks / Pathe / Aardmaan / The Kobal Collection.
P160 *A Midsummer Night's Dream* courtesy of Studio Kresceneho A Loutkoveho Filmu / The Kobal Collection
P163 *Prometheus Bound* courtesy of Peter Dodd – A Manatee Idol Production 2004.
P167 *Sunday Drive* courtesy of José Miguel Ribeiro. © Zeppelin Filmes/S.O.I.L/il Luster/Folimage. Photos by Claudia Guerreiro, Niza and Ana Sequeira.
P171 *The Birth of the Robot* courtesy of Shell-Mex / The Kobal Collection.
P172–173 Dance studies courtesy of David P. France Dance Company.
P175 *War Horse* courtesy of the National Theatre. Photography by Simon Annand.
P177 *Judder* courtesy of Emily Baxter (University of Manitoba).
P177 *Coppélia* courtesy of Birmingham Royal Ballet productions. Photography Bill Cooper. Elisha Willis as Swanhilda and David Morse as Doctor Coppelius.
P180 *(R)evolution* courtesy of Michael Cusack and Anifex Pty Ltd.
P183 *The Typewriter* courtesy of Richard Haynes and Mikolaj Watt.
P184 *Brambly Hedge* © 2009 Hit Entertainment Limited from the Brambly Hedge books by Jill Barklem.
P187 Giordano Ferrari photograph courtesy of *Castello dei Burattini – Museo Giordano Ferrari (Museum of Puppetry, Parma)* in collaboration with IBC Emilia Romagna photographer: Marcello Rossini.

A brief history of stop-motion > **Picture credits** > Acknowledgements

Acknowledgements

For my dear sister Amanda and her husband
Peter who have always helped in so many
ways.

Thanks, too, to all the animators,
marionettists, puppeteers, performers,
producers, dancers, photographers,
craftsmen and artists who have generously
given me permission to use their beautiful
and informative stills.

Finally, thanks to the man who started it all,
Georges Méliès, without whom....

Stop-motion

BASICS
ANIMATION

Working with ethics

Lynne Elvins
Naomi Goulder

Publisher's note

The subject of ethics is not new, yet
its consideration within the applied
visual arts is perhaps not as prevalent
as it might be. Our aim here is to help a
new generation of students, educators
and practitioners find a methodology
for structuring their thoughts and
reflections in this vital area.

AVA Publishing hopes that these
Working with ethics pages provide
a platform for consideration and a
flexible method for incorporating
ethical concerns in the work of
educators, students and professionals.
Our approach consists of four parts:

The **introduction** is intended to be
an accessible snapshot of the ethical
landscape, both in terms of historical
development and current dominant
themes.

The **framework** positions ethical
consideration into four areas and
poses questions about the practical
implications that might occur.
Marking your response to each of
these questions on the scale shown
will allow your reactions to be further
explored by comparison.

The **case study** sets out a real project
and then poses some ethical questions
for further consideration. This is a focus
point for a debate rather than a critical
analysis so there are no predetermined
right or wrong answers.

A selection of **further reading** for you
to consider areas of particular interest in
more detail.

Ethical:
awareness/
reflection/
debate

Working with ethics

Introduction

Ethics is a complex subject that interlaces the idea of responsibilities to society with a wide range of considerations relevant to the character and happiness of the individual. It concerns virtues of compassion, loyalty and strength, but also of confidence, imagination, humour and optimism. As introduced in ancient Greek philosophy, the fundamental ethical question is: *what should I do?* How we might pursue a 'good' life not only raises moral concerns about the effects of our actions on others, but also personal concerns about our own integrity.

In modern times the most important and controversial questions in ethics have been the moral ones. With growing populations and improvements in mobility and communications, it is not surprising that considerations about how to structure our lives together on the planet should come to the forefront. For visual artists and communicators, it should be no surprise that these considerations will enter into the creative process.

Some ethical considerations are already enshrined in government laws and regulations or in professional codes of conduct. For example, plagiarism and breaches of confidentiality can be punishable offences. Legislation in various nations makes it unlawful to exclude people with disabilities from accessing information or spaces. The trade of ivory as a material has been banned in many countries. In these cases, a clear line has been drawn under what is unacceptable.

But most ethical matters remain open to debate, among experts and lay-people alike, and in the end we have to make our own choices on the basis of our own guiding principles or values. Is it more ethical to work for a charity than for a commercial company? Is it unethical to create something that others find ugly or offensive?

Specific questions such as these may lead to other questions that are more abstract. For example, is it only effects on humans (and what they care about) that are important, or might effects on the natural world require attention too?

Is promoting ethical consequences justified even when it requires ethical sacrifices along the way? Must there be a single unifying theory of ethics (such as the Utilitarian thesis that the right course of action is always the one that leads to the greatest happiness of the greatest number), or might there always be many different ethical values that pull a person in various directions?

As we enter into ethical debate and engage with these dilemmas on a personal and professional level, we may change our views or change our view of others. The real test though is whether, as we reflect on these matters, we change the way we act as well as the way we think. Socrates, the 'father' of philosophy, proposed that people will naturally do 'good' if they know what is right. But this point might only lead us to yet another question: *how do we know what is right?*

You
What are your ethical beliefs?

Central to everything you do will be your attitude to people and issues around you. For some people, their ethics are an active part of the decisions they make every day as a consumer, a voter or a working professional. Others may think about ethics very little and yet this does not automatically make them unethical. Personal beliefs, lifestyle, politics, nationality, religion, gender, class or education can all influence your ethical viewpoint.

Using the scale, where would you place yourself? What do you take into account to make your decision? Compare results with your friends or colleagues.

Your client
What are your terms?

Working relationships are central to whether ethics can be embedded into a project, and your conduct on a day-to-day basis is a demonstration of your professional ethics. The decision with the biggest impact is whom you choose to work with in the first place. Cigarette companies or arms traders are often-cited examples when talking about where a line might be drawn, but rarely are real situations so extreme. At what point might you turn down a project on ethical grounds and how much does the reality of having to earn a living affect your ability to choose?

Using the scale, where would you place a project? How does this compare to your personal ethical level?

01 02 03 04 05 06 07 08 09 10

01 02 03 04 05 06 07 08 09 10

Your specifications

What are the impacts of your materials?

In relatively recent times, we are learning that many natural materials are in short supply. At the same time, we are increasingly aware that some man-made materials can have harmful, long-term effects on people or the planet. How much do you know about the materials that you use? Do you know where they come from, how far they travel and under what conditions they are obtained? When your creation is no longer needed, will it be easy and safe to recycle? Will it disappear without a trace? Are these considerations your responsibility or are they out of your hands?

Using the scale, mark how ethical your material choices are.

Your creation

What is the purpose of your work?

Between you, your colleagues and an agreed brief, what will your creation achieve? What purpose will it have in society and will it make a positive contribution? Should your work result in more than commercial success or industry awards? Might your creation help save lives, educate, protect or inspire? Form and function are two established aspects of judging a creation, but there is little consensus on the obligations of visual artists and communicators toward society, or the role they might have in solving social or environmental problems. If you want recognition for being the creator, how responsible are you for what you create and where might that responsibility end?

Using the scale, mark how ethical the purpose of your work is.

01 02 03 04 05 06 07 08 09 10

01 02 03 04 05 06 07 08 09 10

Working with ethics

One aspect of animation that raises an ethical dilemma is that of using the medium to portray inspirational or educational visions that other media might struggle to communicate. Animation has the power to inject life and meaning into futuristic or fantasy settings where cameras cannot go. With it comes the ability to help audiences see a different way of thinking. It also has the capacity to take even the most difficult or disturbing subjects and handle them in ways that make them watchable. Is it the responsibility of animators to always approach the medium with a sense of gravity about what it might achieve in the minds of viewers? Are less serious intentions always shallow and therefore less important, or is there a legitimate role for pure entertainment or escapism?

Fritz the Cat was a comic-strip character created by Robert Crumb, an American artist and illustrator recognised for his distinctive style, and critical and subversive view of the American mainstream. Fritz first appeared in print during the height of the 1960s Underground Comix Movement, of which Crumb is regarded as one of the most prominent figures. As the Fritz character developed he became a parody of middle-class bohemians who professed to be seeking cosmic truths when they were actually more interested in chasing women.

The idea for making a feature-length film happened when producer Steve Krantz came across some of the stories. Krantz and director Ralph Bakshi got in touch with Crumb to discuss the film rights. The animated film is a satire on 1960s college life, race relations, the Free Love Movement and politics. It focuses on Fritz, who explores the ideals of hedonism as he participates in major social upheavals based around the Student Protest Movement of the time. Released to theatres in 1972, the film was the first ever animation to be X-rated. The plot includes various anthropomorphic characters involved in group sex, taking drugs, stealing cars, riots, rape, domestic violence and the deliberate bombing of a power plant.

Bakshi is said to have wanted the film to be the antithesis of the Walt Disney productions and included two satirical references to Disney. In one, silhouettes of Mickey Mouse, Minnie Mouse and Donald Duck are shown cheering on the US Air Force as it drops napalm on a black neighbourhood during a riot. Two female animators are said to have quit, one because she could not bring herself to tell her children what she was doing for a living, the other because she refused to draw exposed breasts.

Crumb is said to have disliked the film so much that he filed suit to have his name removed from the credits. However, as his name has remained, it is not known if this is true. Despite Crumb's objections, *Fritz the Cat* was a box office hit. Made for under USD$1 million, it was the first independent animated film to gross more than USD$100 million. But Crumb's displeasure with the film led him to kill the character and stop the production of any future films.

Is it more ethical to use animated characters, rather than real actors, to portray scenes of sex or violence?

Is it unethical to develop a story without involving the writer?

Would you have worked on *Fritz the Cat*?

Animation can explain whatever the mind of man can conceive. This facility makes it the most versatile and explicit means of communication yet devised for quick mass appreciation.

Walt Disney

Working with ethics

Further reading

AIGA
Design Business and Ethics
2007, AIGA

Eaton, Marcia Muelder
Aesthetics and the Good Life
1989, Associated University Press

Ellison, David
Ethics and Aesthetics in European Modernist Literature:
From the Sublime to the Uncanny
2001, Cambridge University Press

Fenner, David E W (Ed)
Ethics and the Arts:
An Anthology
1995, Garland Reference Library of Social Science

Gini, Al and Marcoux, Alexei M
Case Studies in Business Ethics
2005, Prentice Hall

McDonough, William and Braungart, Michael
Cradle to Cradle:
Remaking the Way We Make Things
2002, North Point Press

Papanek, Victor
Design for the Real World:
Making to Measure
1972, Thames & Hudson

United Nations Global Compact
The Ten Principles
www.unglobalcompact.org/AboutTheGC/TheTenPrinciples/index.html